WILLIAMS-SONOMA

FLORENCE

AUTHENTIC RECIPES CELEBRATING THE FOODS OF THE WORLD

Recipes and Text
LORI DE MORI

Photographs
JASON LOWE

General Editor
CHUCK WILLIAMS

Oxmoor
House

INTRODUCTION

13 Culinary History

14 Contemporary Cuisine

16 Dining Out

23 Markets

26 Map of Florence and Tuscany

BEST OF FLORENCE

30 SALUMI AND AFFETTATI

34 TUSCAN OLIVE OIL

38 CAFÉS

44 TUSCAN WINE

53 ARTISAN BREAD

56 ARTISAN CHEESE

62 GELATO

REFERENCE

185 Glossary

187 Ingredient Sources

188 Index

191 Acknowledgments and
     Photography Locations

CONTENTS

RECIPES

ANTIPASTI

70 FRITTATA DI PORRI E ZUCCHINI
Leek and Zucchini Frittata

73 BRUSCHETTE CON CANNELLINI
E OLIO NUOVO
Bruschetta with White Beans and Olive Oil

74 INSALATA DI GALLINA
Poached Chicken Salad with Spicy Mayonnaise

77 PROSCIUTTO, SALAME, MELONE E FICCHI
Prosciutto, Salami, Melon, and Figs

78 TORTA SALATA CON BIETOLA
Savory Tart with Swiss Chard

81 INSALATA GARGA
Arugula Salad with Pine Nuts, Avocado,
and Hearts of Palm

82 CARCIOFI SOTT'OLIO
Marinated Artichoke Hearts

82 OLIVE INSAPORITE
Spicy Black and Green Olives

85 SCHIACCIATA AL RAMERINO E SALVIA
Flatbread with Rosemary and Sage

86 CROSTINI DI FEGATINI DI POLLO
Chicken Liver Crostini

89 INSALATA DI BACCELLI E PECORINO
Fava Bean and Pecorino Cheese Salad

PRIMI

94 PIZZA CON MOZZARELLA, CIPOLLA E RUCOLA
Pizza with Mozzarella, Onion, and Arugula

97 FARRO CON CALAMARETTI, RUCOLA
E POMODORI CILIEGINI
Farro with Squid, Arugula, and
Cherry Tomatoes

98 PENNE CON PESCE SPADA E MELANZANE
Penne with Swordfish and Eggplant

101 TAGLIATELLE AI FUNGHI PORCINI
Tagliatelle with Porcino Mushrooms

102 RAVIOLI DI RICOTTA CON POMODORI
Ricotta Ravioli with Fresh Tomatoes

105 PANZANELLA
Bread Salad

106 LINGUINE A' MASANIELLO
Linguine with Shellfish

109 GNUDI DI RICOTTA E SPINACI AL TARTUFO
Ricotta and Spinach Dumplings
with Truffles

110 PAPPA AL POMODORO
Tomato and Bread Soup

113 RISOTTO AL SALTO ALLA PARMIGIANA
IN SALSA DI ZAFFERANO
Parmesan Risotto Cakes with
Saffron Sauce

114 CREMA DI CECI CON FARRO
E FUNGHI PORCINI
Puréed Chickpea Soup with Farro
and Porcino Mushrooms

117 POLENTA CON RAGÙ DI CARNE
Polenta with Beef Ragù

118 RIBOLLITA
Twice-Cooked Vegetable Soup

SECONDI

125 BOCCONCINI DI VITELLA AL
RABARBARO E MIELE
Veal with Rhubarb-Honey Sauce

126 POLLO ARROSTO AL LIMONE
Lemon Roasted Chicken

129 TAGLIATA DI MANZO
Grilled Florentine Steak

130 FILETTI DI ROMBO AL FORNO
CON CARCIOFI
Baked Turbot with Artichokes

133 SCAMERITA COL CAVOLO NERO
Pork with Tuscan Black Cabbage

134 STRACOTTO AL PÈPPOLI
Braised Beef with Pèppoli Wine

137 CONIGLIO CON OLIVE E PINOLI
Rabbit with Olives and Pine Nuts

138 COSTOLETTE D'AGNELLO AI PEPI
Lamb Chops with Mixed Peppercorns

141 BACCALÀ ALLA FIORENTINA
Salt Cod, Florentine Style

142 OSSOBUCO ALLA FIORENTINA
Osso Buco, Florentine Style

CONTORNI

149 PEPERONATA
Braised Sweet Peppers, Tomatoes,
and Onions

150 ASPARAGI CON UOVO E PARMIGIANO
Asparagus with Fried Eggs and Parmesan

153 ZUCCHINI TRIFOLATI
Zucchini with Olive Oil, Garlic, and Parsley

154 FAGIOLI ALL'UCCELLETTO
White Beans in Tomato Sauce

157 PISELLI SGRANATI CON CIPOLLA E BASILICO
Freshly Shucked Peas with Onion and Basil

158 CARCIOFI E PATATE BRASATI
Braised Artichokes and Potatoes

161 SPINACI ALL'AGRO
Spinach with Lemon and Olive Oil

DOLCI

167 SORBETTO DI PESCA
Peach Sorbet

168 GELATO DI CREMA AL PROFUMO DI CAFFÈ
Coffee-Scented Custard Gelato

171 CROSTATA DI LAMPONI
Raspberry Tart

172 TORTA DI MELE CON CREMA ALL'INGLESE
Apple Torte with Custard Cream

175 TORTA DI FICHI E NOCI
Fig and Walnut Torte

176 CIOCCOLATA CALDA CON PANNA MONTATA
Thick Hot Chocolate with Whipped Cream

179 MACEDONIA DI FRUTTA
Fruit Salad

180 BISCOTTINI DI PRATO
Almond Biscotti

183 FRITTELLE DI PERE
Pear Fritters

INTRODUCTION

The food of Florence speaks much about the city's soul. The artisans behind it—cheese makers, bakers, winemakers, chefs—are inspiring masters of their crafts in a world where all too often such skills have been forgotten and the sense of connection between *la terra* (the land) and how it nourishes us has been lost.

CULINARY HISTORY

To say that the city of Florence has been given more than its fair share of beauty and genius is not an exaggeration. Leonardo da Vinci and Michelangelo painted and sculpted there; Dante and Boccaccio wrote; Galileo explored the heavens; and the Medici family ruled with an unparalleled devotion to culture and the arts. But there is another way to understand Florence—through the scent of unsalted bread, the fruity tang of jewel green olive oil, the frugality of a winter soup made with cabbage and day-old bread, the delight of freshly shucked fava (broad) beans with milky white sheep's milk cheese, or a bottle of wine from the neighboring hills shared over a languorous lunch.

Historically, Florentine cooking has two bloodlines, as different from each other as night and day—the opulent cuisine of the aristocracy and wealthy merchant class, and the simple, unrefined cooking of the peasants and laborers. What strange irony it is that the second of the two not only has survived but also has come to symbolize gastronomic excellence throughout the world.

At no time in history were culinary theatrics taken to a greater extreme than in Florence during the Renaissance under the Medici family rule. The politically unified Italy as we know it today did not yet exist. Instead, "Italy" was a collection of fractious city-states, constantly at odds with one another and, if not actually warring, at the very least doing their best to impress and intimidate their neighbors. The unprecedented explosion of literary and artistic genius during this time was manifested especially in Florence. As a result, a feast or banquet was not merely a meal, but also a chance to display wealth, worldliness, and artistry.

Maria de' Medici's nuptial feast was held in the Palazzo Vecchio's Sala del Cinquecento, sumptuously frescoed by the court painter Vasari and his studio. There were giant sugar sculptures by Giambologna (whose *Rape of the Sabines* still stands under the Loggia dei Lanzi outside the Palazzo Vecchio); smaller fruit, sugar, and butter sculptures on the tables; napkins folded into the shapes of animals; and what seemed like an infinity of

courses (interspersed with elaborately staged theatrical performances), including a cooked swan redressed in its feathers and gliding upon a lake of wine, steaming pies filled with sweetbreads, and pastry-covered pâtés shaped to look like unicorns and hydras.

To this day, Florentines are convinced that the origins of fine French cooking are directly attributable to Catherine de' Medici's move to France upon her marriage to King Henry II. But though dishes such as *anatra all'arancia* (duck in orange sauce), originally a Tuscan recipe, have survived on some local menus, Florentines seem happy enough to let France keep its haute cuisine, while they continue to enjoy the foods of their humbler ancestors.

What are those foods? First and foremost they are *pane, olio e vino*—bread, olive oil, and wine. In fact, in the old days of the Tuscan countryside, dinner was usually *pane e companatico*—bread and something to go with the bread—and an afternoon *merenda*, or snack, was likely to be simply a slice of bread sprinkled with sugar and moistened with a bit of rustic red wine. This frugality

was neither sad nor oppressive, for even when circumstances made for a modest life, it was rarely a bleak or colorless one.

Florence is located in the northern part of Tuscany, a region with a landscape as diverse as it is beautiful, encompassing the sparkling Mediterranean Sea, white marbled mountains, thickly wooded forests, meandering rivers, and fertile rolling hills. Tuscany's temperate climate had a direct effect on its cuisine, since it supported the raising of livestock and

growing of food year-round. The land also gave freely of its uncultivated gifts: mushrooms; blackberries; edible nettles; lettuces; boar, hare, and pheasant.

The straightforward simplicity of Florentine cooking has evolved over hundreds of years, with its humble beginnings, noble influences, and fertile surroundings all playing a part. The flavors underlying it are pure, essential, and at their best when left to sing in their own clear voices. And sing they do.

CONTEMPORARY CUISINE

The cuisine of Florence has changed little over the years—for good reason. The city boasts a selection of locally grown ingredients and artisan food products second to none, and its residents possess a deep-rooted respect for culinary tradition.

There is a habit in Italy, and Florence is no exception, of talking about food while eating—"wonderful meals I've eaten" being a particularly frequent topic. If you ask a Florentine how important food is in the grand scheme of life, chances are he or she will look at you askance and respond, "What do you mean? It is *essential*…as important as air and water." In other words, so important that its importance is not even open to discussion.

Words like *nostrale* and *genuino* are music to the Florentine palate. *Nostrale* is a word you'll see written in bold print on a scrap of cardboard alongside a basket of summer zucchini (courgettes) or *pomodori* (tomatoes). From *nostro,* meaning "ours," it indicates locally grown, and implicit in that label is the belief that the food will be superior to anything else of its kind available. (Of course, food grown in one's own backyard is better still.)

Genuino or *genuinità* refers to genuineness and authenticity and is more of a concept than a label. Bread leavened with natural yeast and baked in a wood-burning oven is *genuino*, as is cheese from the milk of sheep that graze on wild Tuscan grasses, or the oil from your neighbor's olives, picked by hand each autumn and taken to the local mill to be pressed. Where there is *genuinità* there are likely to be *artigiani*—the passionate, hardworking artisans whose abiding respect for tradition and the land keep alive such ancient crafts as the curing of meat and the making of cheese, wine, and bread.

Florentines are not impressed by produce that has traveled from faraway continents in another hemisphere. They have little desire to eat peaches in winter or porcino mushrooms foraged in foreign woods. Instead, they have faith, take pleasure in the fruits of their own

gentle hills and valleys, and maintain an appreciation of the many gifts of each season: spring's asparagus, artichokes, cherries, and strawberries; summer's tomatoes, eggplants (aubergines), melons, and plums; autumn's mushrooms, freshly pressed olive oil, figs, and grapes; and winter's squash, persimmons, chestnuts, and dark Tuscan cabbage known as *cavolo nero*.

Autumn brings the Florentine countryside to its most lush level of abundance. First is *la vendemmia,* the grape harvest. The vineyards swarm with grape pickers and tractors ferrying grapes to be crushed, and a faint smell of must hangs in the air after the pressing. While the ancient alchemy that turns grape juice into wine is at work, rickety wooden ladders are propped up against olive trees and wide nets are spread below their branches for the olive harvest. *Olio nuovo*—just-pressed olive oil—is the most eagerly awaited culinary event of the year, celebrated simply, as is the Tuscan way, by drenching toasted bread or creamy cannellini beans with the sharp,

fruity oil and endlessly comparing the merits of this year's oil to last year's.

Another benchmark of Florentine cooking is frugality. The cuisine is not a mean or parsimonious one as much as it is a series of naturally efficient habits so ingrained in the culinary consciousness as to render the notion of frugality almost invisible. Soups and salads are made from stale bread—*ribollita, pappa al pomodoro*, and *panzanella* being the most famous. Bakers cook beans in the cooling ovens once the bread making is done, and potters use the glimmering embers from their kilns to make *peposo alla fornacina,* a hearty mixture of beef, garlic, peppercorns, and wine, stewed for hours and then eaten with bread and red wine.

Despite the enormous weight of tradition, the rhythms of modern life unquestionably have crept into the city. Gone for the most part is the daily two-hour lunch replete with *antipasto, primo, secondo, contorno, dolce,* a generous carafe of *vino,* and a short nap to round out the afternoon. Nevertheless,

the typical Florentine day, gastronomically speaking, has its well-established paces, and the city's denizens continue to do justice to that enviable notion of *la bella vita. La prima colazione,* or breakfast, at a *bar* (café) or at home, is little more than a caffe latte or cappuccino and a bun, with a second *caffè* at a *bar* at midmorning. *Il pranzo,* or lunch, consists of *una minestra* (a soup, Florentines being very partial to soups), *una bella pastasciutta* (a nice pasta), or perhaps *una fettina di carne* (a small slice of beef or pork), and *un'insalata* or a piece of fruit served on a plate and carefully peeled and sliced with a knife. The young and hip might stop at a *bar* for an *aperitivo* before dinner. *La cena,* or dinner, has remained sacrosanct— whether at home with the family gathered around the table or *al ristorante,* it is, without a doubt, Florence at its most civilized.

A trattoria meal will almost always begin with a platter of *affettati* (cured meats such as prosciutto, *salame,* and fennel-scented *finocchiona*) and *crostini de fegatini* (chicken

liver–pâté crostini), followed by a *primo* such as a bread soup or pasta with ragù (meat sauce), peas, zucchini, mushrooms, artichokes, or any other seasonable vegetable. Main courses typically are grilled meats *(carne alla brace),* roasted meats such as *arista* (pork with rosemary and garlic), braised beef *(stracotto),* or chicken or rabbit, fricasséed or dipped in batter and fried. Squid or cuttlefish in *zimino* (cooked with tomatoes, Swiss chard, and *peperoncino*) is a favorite seafood dish, as is *baccalà* (salt cod) cooked with plum (Roma) tomatoes,

which is typically offered on Friday menus. The most common *contorni,* or side dishes, are stewed white beans, sautéed spinach or chard, roasted potatoes, and *insalata verde* (green salad). That said, most restaurants will also serve a highly seasonal *contorno* such as fresh peas in spring, braised sweet red bell peppers (capsicums) in summer, or *funghi porcini* (porcino mushrooms) in autumn. After such a meal, dessert will most certainly be *biscottini di Prato,* hard almond biscuits to dip in the locally made sweet, golden wine called *vin santo.*

DINING OUT

One of the best ways to sample many of Florence's most beloved recipes, some bearing the well-worn cloak of tradition and others the sleek stamp of innovation, is in its time-honored trattorias, casual wine bars, and elegant restaurants.

When is a *ristorante* not a restaurant? When it's an *osteria* or a trattoria. In the past these monikers held more importance than they do today. Historically an *osteria* was a rustic, tavernlike place to stop for a glass of local wine and some simple food. Next on the food chain was the trattoria—most tended to be family-run and had menus consisting primarily of traditional dishes served in a homey atmosphere. Finally came the *ristorante:* more sophisticated and more costly, with haute cuisine, hotelier-level staff, and dishes that ventured outside the traditional repertoire of local specialties.

Today such labels tend to be more confusing than descriptive. Florence's Osteria del Caffè Italiano is a smart and stylish place serving elegant interpretations of local cuisine.

Many trattorias are so-called simply because they bear the name bestowed on them by their original family owners, sometimes up to a century ago. The best bet is to ask locals about places that sound interesting to you, or to take a peek into a restaurant and look at its menu before making a reservation.

When dining in Florence, you should keep a few practices in mind. Mealtimes may be later than what you may be accustomed to in the United States and elsewhere. *Pranzo,* or lunch, is from 1:00 p.m. to about 2:30 p.m., and *cena,* or dinner, from 7:30 p.m. until 10:30 p.m. Simple eateries do not always have printed menus; expect the waiter to recite the menu at the table. Coffee is served after dessert rather than with it, and a cappuccino is considered a breakfast

or snack beverage, *never* something that concludes a meal. Finally, in Italy, it is customary not to rush diners through a meal. Consequently, your waiter will not bring your bill to the table until you ask for it.

Classic Tuscan Restaurants

Among the best classic restaurants in Florence is Sostanza, which first opened in 1869. Sostanza inspires a fierce loyalty in its customers, both locals and those who arrive with guidebooks in hand or with notes from friends who have told them exactly what they should eat: dishes like *bistecca alla fiorentina,* a giant slab of beef grilled in the fireplace that dominates the restaurant's tiny kitchen, or *tortino di carciofi,* an astonishing and beautiful artichoke omelet shaped into a swirl so delicate you may not believe that it, too, was cooked in a frying pan over the embers of a wood fire.

Coco Lezzone is one of the few Florentine restaurants that seriously rivals Sostanza's reputation for unreservedly traditional Florentine food. Its waiters speak disappointingly good English, owing to the flocks of tourists who come from far and wide to sit at tables covered with red-and-white-checked tablecloths and sample the mainstays of Florentine cooking. Cynics suspecting the place of being more hype than substance would be well advised to step into the kitchen for a look at the ancient wood-burning stove responsible for churning out the deliciously authentic Florentine food.

Less well known but a favorite among locals and savvy travelers is the tiny Buca dell'Orafo, near the Ponte Vecchio, the city's famed "old bridge," which spans the Arno River. Since 1945, Buca dell'Orafo has served the sort of uncompromisingly straightforward, seasonal food that is the hallmark of Florentine cooking.

Many of the city's most delightful classic restaurants are on the edge of town or just outside. The restaurant Omero, set among the posh villas of Arcetri, is just minutes from the city, but has all the quiet and serenity of the countryside. The airy dining room has views of the green hills of Florence dotted with farmhouses, olive trees, and vineyards. The place serves everything one would expect to find on a Florentine menu—including crostini, *affettati, ribollita,* grilled meats, and the ubiquitous *biscottini di Prato*—all impeccably presented and prepared. On Monte Morello, another hilltop overlooking the city, Trattoria I Ricchi also adheres to tradition. Meals can be enjoyed here on a leafy terrace, and the hospitality is as generous and comforting as the food itself.

Trendsetting Restaurants

Culturally as well as culinarily, Florentines are conservatives and traditionalists. And why not, you might ask: They are, after all, beneficiaries of one of the richest cultural heritages of all time. They tend to like what they know, are reassured by the familiar, and gravitate toward that which has survived the exacting test of time. As a result, change, innovation, and originality are more likely to be met with

a raised eyebrow of skepticism than wide-eyed enthusiasm. This can be more than a little disheartening for those who would rather answer to their own muse than stick to the well-trodden path of tradition. However, a handful of brave restaurateurs have done just that, conquering Florentine diffidence with a skill and determination that have made them heroes of the city's gastronomic scene.

First is Fabio Picchi, the man behind the Cibrèo restaurant, trattoria, and café and the new Teatro del Sale, a cultural and theatrical space nestled among the Cibrèo eateries that he opened with his wife, the actress Maria Cassi. He is immensely talented, with the uncompromising temperament of an artist, and has succeeded in both reviving and reinventing traditional Florentine cooking.

Florentine by adoption but from the southern Italian region of Basilicata by birth, Umberto Montana created Alle Murate, a restaurant with an intimately lit dining room where sultry jazz plays in the background. Alle Murate features the inspired cooking of

Giovanna Iorio and offers two tasting menus: one "creative" (often containing Basilicata specialties) and the other traditionally Tuscan.

When David Gardner opened trattoria-pizzeria Baldovino in 1995, he had three strikes against him: he was young, he was Scottish, and he had no background in the restaurant business. Since then, he has become one of the city's most dynamic restaurateurs, going on to open the Enoteca Baldovino wine bar and the stylish, upmarket Beccofino restaurant.

Ethnic Florence

Until only recently, Florence's restaurants mirrored the resolutely old-world, tradition-bound nature of the city. Yes, the food was outstanding—but it was also predictable to an extreme. Food lovers looking for a change of flavors were likely to find themselves thumbing through cookbooks and trying to figure out where to buy coconut milk for a Thai curry or whether polenta from the Veneto could be used to make Mexican tortillas.

Over the past few decades, however, a refreshing worldliness has crept into the city. In the Etruscan hilltown of Fiésole, with its impossibly beautiful views of the city, the restaurant India has conjured a taste of the great subcontinent. Ramraj Rosticerria Indiana on Via Ghibellina, with its clay tandoor and the generous smiles of owner Reddy Rema and her daughter, Pratna, has done the same. You will also find Ruth's, a kosher vegetarian restaurant next to the city's stunning copper-domed synagogue; Rose's for sushi; and a smattering of Egyptian falafel shops scattered throughout town. Sésame, whose sensuous garden is like something out of *The Arabian Nights,* is the place to go for Moroccan couscous or just to drape yourself decorously on a chaise longue, sipping mint tea out of filigreed glasses.

Florentine cuisine is still going strong within this expanding culinary landscape—and it may taste all the better when you've had the chance to step away from it for a meal or two.

MARKETS

Not having your own kitchen while visiting Florence is no excuse to miss taking a trip to at least one of the city's outstanding markets. In addition to the simple pleasure of beholding such glorious abundance, you will certainly find no better way to understand the particular delights each Tuscan season brings.

There are a number of ways to *fare la spesa* (do the grocery shopping) in Florence. The city has two covered markets, the Mercato Centrale in the San Lorenzo district (open Monday through Friday from 7 a.m. to 2 p.m.; Saturdays from 7 a.m. to 2 p.m. and again from 4 p.m. until 7 p.m.) and the Mercato di Sant'Ambrogio, not far from Piazza Santa Croce (open Monday through Saturday from 7 a.m. to 2 p.m.).

The Mercato Centrale is the city's largest market, an enormous turn-of-the-century structure made of cast iron and glass, housing an infinity of stalls. Downstairs are the *gastronomie,* or delicatessens, selling prepared foods, breads, cured meats, and cheeses. Here, too, are the butchers, some of whom specialize in poultry and rabbit, others in offal, including tripe. Still others offer every conceivable cut of beef and other favorite meats in wide glass cases, some already neatly rolled, tied with kitchen string, seasoned, and ready for the oven. Upstairs are the market's fruit and vegetable vendors, as well as specialty stands selling a variety of dried fruits, olives, and culinary herbs.

The Mercato di Sant'Ambrogio is smaller than the Mercato Centrale. All of the market's meats, breads, and *gastronomie,* as well as a wonderful cafeteria, are indoors, while the greengrocers, florists, and a smattering of housewares and clothing stands are situated outside under a covered portico.

Other shoppers choose to market in the many (mostly family-owned) specialty shops scattered throughout the city. Most neighborhoods have a bustling shopping street. A full marketing trip will require stops at the *forno* or *panificio* (bakery); *macelleria* (butcher shop); *pescheria* or *pescivendolo* (fishmonger); *latteria* (dairy); *ortolano* or *fruttivendolo* (greengrocer); and *alimentare, gastronomia,* or *pizzicagnolo* (for cured meats, cheeses, and various and sundry items not sold in the other shops). A welcome addition to the marketing spectrum are the well-stocked Asian markets in Piazza Santa Maria Novella and near the Mercato di San Lorenzo, which sell an impressive variety of rice, legumes, and spices, and even hard-to-find herbs like fresh lemongrass.

The timetable by which the specialty shops operate can be daunting to learn at first— they are generally closed for lunch between the hours of 1 p.m. and somewhere around 4 p.m., and they keep summer hours and winter hours (most shops are closed on Saturday afternoons during summer and on Wednesday afternoons in winter). Additionally, fishmongers are open only in the mornings, and butcher shops are typically closed on Thursday afternoons.

Those seeking convenience rather than the singular pleasure of establishing a relationship with individual shopkeepers and purveyors of particular foods head to the ever-increasing

battery of supermarkets on the edge of the city. Even these are still, to some extent, a collection of markets within a market. In addition to the aisles of dried and canned goods, there are separate counters for the butcher, delicatessen, and fishmonger. The experience is different from supermarkets in the United States in that you don disposable plastic gloves while choosing, weighing, and applying the price tags to your own vegetables, and you bag your own groceries.

You may also encounter a *sagra,* a food festival dedicated to a particular food or dish. *Sagre* are particularly common in the countryside surrounding Florence, where they are held to celebrate everything from porcino mushrooms, truffles, and homemade stuffed pasta to wild boar, sheep's milk cheese, and even onions. Finally, there are the weekly *mercati.* At the Tuesday-morning market at Le Cascine park (page 149), fruit, vegetable, and houseware stands are set up alongside rotisserie stalls with rows of chickens roasting on spits, deep-fried polenta and potato

croquettes, and whole roast pigs *(porchetta)* that are carved into sandwiches. Monthly organic *fierucola* or *fierucolona* markets (page 157) are held in Piazza Santo Spirito or Piazza della Santissima Annunziata.

It is fascinating to observe the dialogue between shopper and shopkeeper in the Florentine marketplace. You might be surprised to see greengrocers selecting fruits and vegetables from the various baskets and bins for their customers. Don't be concerned— they wouldn't dare risk losing a customer by trying to pass off produce past its prime. You may be equally surprised to hear how often vendors give cooking suggestions to their customers or want to know how their patrons plan on cooking whatever they are buying. For example, a greengrocer wouldn't sell you the same artichokes for cooking as for eating raw, and a fishmonger will suggest particular fish varieties for children and others for adults.

In an average transaction in a Florentine market, just about everything from a loaf of

bread to a pound of tomatoes is chosen with the utmost specificity. There are those who like their bread *cotto bene* (well cooked) and those who look for a lighter crust, those who prefer their salad tomatoes *maturi* (ripe and red) and those who like them tart and still partially green. It is a dialogue both sides seem to expect and enjoy, and one you will be encouraged to engage in should you want to do some marketing.

And why not—the Boboli Gardens and the tree-lined Piazza Santo Spirito and Piazza D'Azeglio are perfect spots for a picnic. Buy a crusty loaf of bread baked in a wood-burning oven; some sliced *prosciutto crudo* and *finocchiona* (soft local salami flavored with fennel seeds); a tub of spicy green olives; a wedge of fresh pecorino cheese and a pound of unshelled fava (broad) beans to eat along with it; and a bag of ripe cherries for dessert. Add a knife, a small bottle of olive oil, a large bottle of wine, and a hungry companion with whom to share your feast, and soon you'll be ready to explore the city once again.

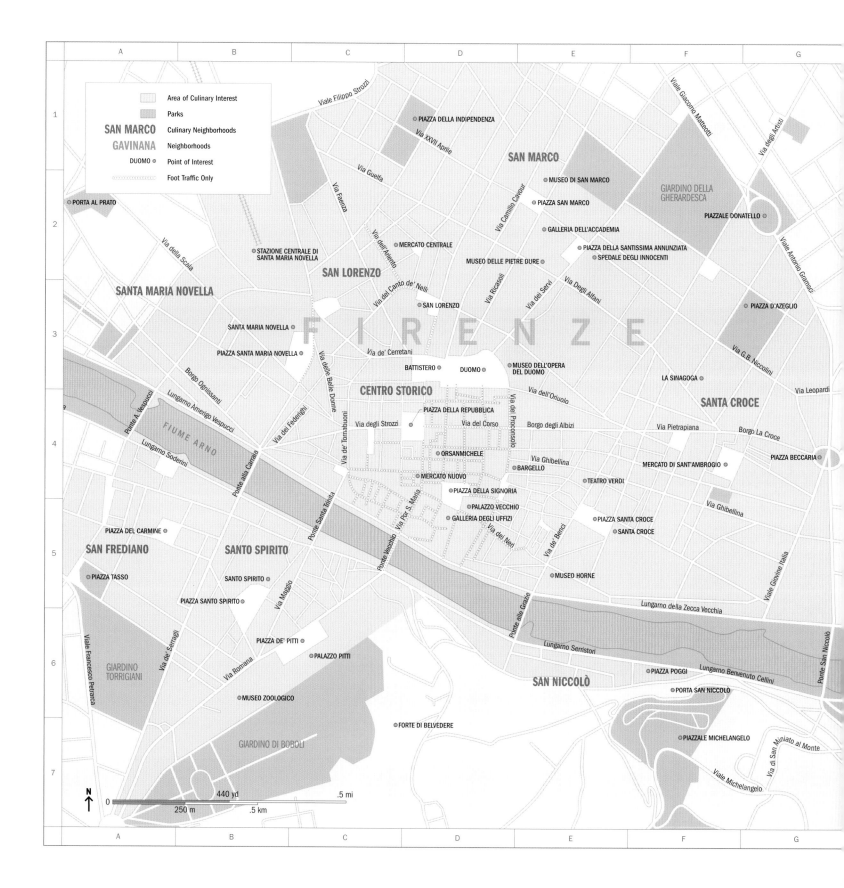

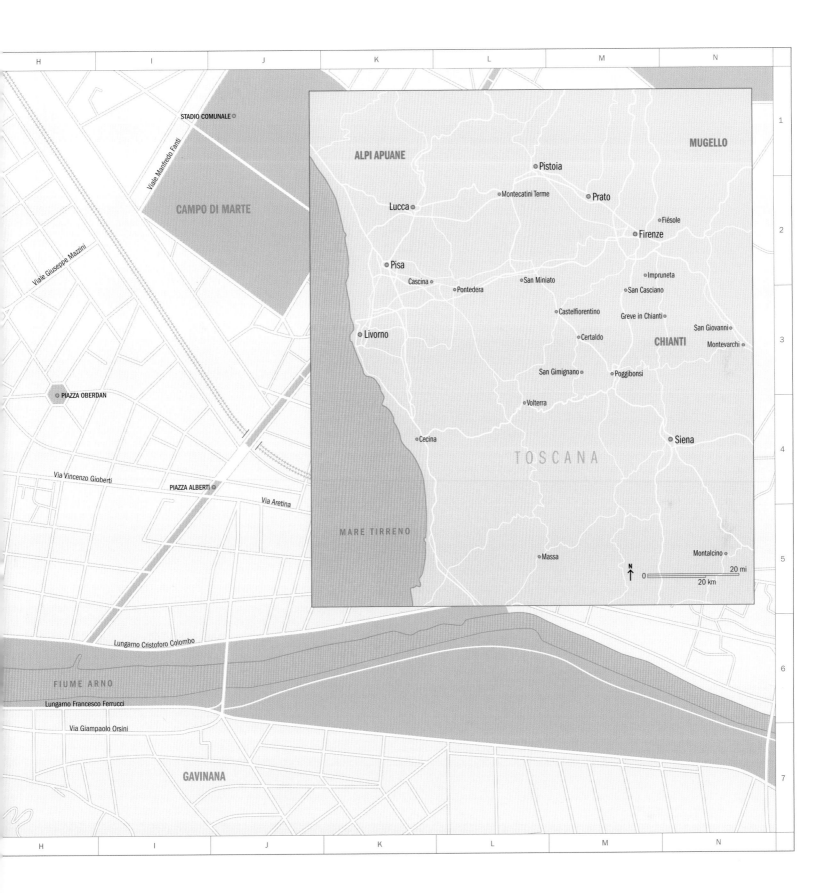

STADIO COMUNALE

CAMPO DI MARTE

Viale Manfredo Fanti

Viale Giuseppe Mazzini

PIAZZA OBERDAN

Via Vincenzo Gioberti

PIAZZA ALBERTI

Via Aretina

Lungarno Cristoforo Colombo

FIUME ARNO

Lungarno Francesco Ferrucci

Via Giampaolo Orsini

GAVINANA

ALPI APUANE

MUGELLO

Pistoia

Montecatini Terme

Prato

Lucca

Fiésole

Firenze

Pisa

Impruneta

Cascina

San Miniato

San Casciano

Pontedera

Castelfiorentino

Greve in Chianti

Livorno

San Giovanni

Certaldo

CHIANTI

Montevarchi

San Gimignano

Poggibonsi

Volterra

Siena

TOSCANA

Cecina

MARE TIRRENO

Massa

Montalcino

N

0   20 mi
      20 km

Best of **FLORENCE**

The curing of pork has been an established art in Tuscany since the Middle Ages. The first laws regulating the process of production were laid down in the fifteenth century. Technological advances notwithstanding, these practices have changed very little.

SALUMI AND AFFETTATI

In Tuscany there is still truth to the old saying, "Dal porco, non si getta niente, tutto è squisito" (Nothing is thrown away from a pig, all is delicious). Traditionally, anyone with a bit of land made room for a *porcile* (pigsty), and once a year, usually during winter, the *norcino* (pork butcher)—the best came from the Umbrian town of Norcia—arrived to ply his trade. Nothing was wasted, though much had to be preserved in a way that would keep the family well fed for months. *Sale* (salt) was the answer, which resulted in the many time-honored Italian preparations of cured meats. Though fewer and fewer people today raise their own livestock, modernity has done little to dull Italy's taste for *salumi,* the cured pork products that still begin many a meal.

Imagine this scene: A handful of people settle around a table in a traditional Florentine trattoria. The waiter comes, eyes the group, draws an oval in the air with his finger, and says, part question, part affirmation, "Affettati misti,"—meaning, "Shall I bring a plate of cured meats to the table while you all decide what to eat?" The answer will almost always be a resounding yes.

There will be *prosciutto crudo,* cured ham—either *dolce* or *salato,* the former usually from Parma or San Daniele in the north of Italy, the latter *toscano,* that is, local. *Dolce* in this case doesn't mean sweet so much as mild and less salty. Prosciutto from Parma is moist and delicate with a sweet earthiness; *prosciutto toscano* is dark, drier, and salty, wonderfully suited for Tuscan bread, which is usually unsalted. Prosciutto is most often cut to an almost translucent thinness in a meat slicer, but many enthusiasts prefer it cut by hand.

Next will be salami, usually at least two types—typically *toscano,* a rich and firm *salame* seasoned with garlic, peppercorns, and wine and flecked with creamy white chunks of fat; and *finocchiona* or *sbriciolona,* large, crumbly, coarse-grained salami laced with peppercorns and wild fennel seeds. There may also be *coppa* (made from the pig's neck), *spalla* (from the shoulder), or the humble but much-loved *soppressata,* made from the head and lesser prized parts of the pig and eaten fresh rather than aged.

When shopping for cured meats in Florence, visit Perini, inside the Mercato Centrale, which has a fine selection. Other markets and shops also sell cured meats: Alla Botteghina dell'Augusta in the Mercato di Sant'Ambrogio, Anzuini on Via dei Neri, and Grana Market on Via dei Tavolini.

The cured meats of Tuscany are among some of the best loved in Italy.

SALAME TOSCANO

SALAME DI CINGHIALE

PROSCIUTTO DOLCE

FINOCCHIONA

SALAME TOSCANO

The word *salame* derives from the Latin *sal* (salt), salami's traditional preservative. Tuscan salami are made from the lean meat of mature pigs, finely ground and mixed with small cubes of pork lard and peppercorns. A portion of the pig's intestine is used as a casing for the mixture, hence the term *insaccati* (literally "put into a sack") used to refer to sausages and salami in general. The fresh salami are hung in an aging room for about two months to dry and season.

SALAME DI CINGHIALE

Cinghiali, "wild boar," live in the woods throughout Tuscany. It is not uncommon to come upon a pair of sows and their young walking nose to tail through the woods. They are mythical-looking creatures with dark bristly hair and improbably long, pointed snouts, which they use to sniff out the roots and herbs they like to eat. *Cinghiale* is also a favorite game meat. It is slowly braised when fresh or made into deeply flavored prosciutti, *salame,* and *salsicce* (sausages).

PROSCIUTTO DOLCE

All prosciutti, whether *dolce* (sweet) or *salato* (salted), are made from the hind thigh of a pig just under a year old. Delicately flavored *prosciutto di Parma* comes from pigs fed, among other things, whey left over from the Parmigiano-Reggiano cheese-making process. *Prosciutto di San Daniele* is pressed into a distinctive violin-like shape, while Parma prosciutti are rounder. Both have dense, red meat and creamy, white fat, and are considered *dolce* in Florence, where the local *prosciutto toscano* is more salty (see right).

FINOCCHIONA

Finocchiona is an aged *salame* made from minced pork belly and jowl seasoned with wine and fennel. The verb *infinocchiare* means "to cheat" or "to swindle," and adopting the word as the name of this sausage dates back to the days when farmers sold *vino sfuso* (unbottled wine) and offered prospective buyers slices of *salame* with fennel seeds, whose delicious aniselike flavor interferes with the ability to taste wine. As a result, an inferior wine tasted better than it really was.

PROSCIUTTO TOSCANO

SOPPRESSATA

SALSICCIA DI CINTA SENESE

SBRICIOLONA

PROSCIUTTO TOSCANO

While the rest of Italy shows a slight preference for the more delicate *prosciutto dolce* of the north, salty *prosciutto toscano* is Florence's favorite. The making of *prosciutto toscano* is an age-old art. The fresh hams are refrigerated so that the meat hardens, then are cleaned, shaped, and salt-cured in aging rooms. *Prosciutto toscano,* made at private farms in the countryside, is often boned before curing to facilitate aging and storage.

SOPPRESSATA

Soppressata (also known as *coppa di testa*) is Tuscany's most humble *insaccato* (see *salame toscano,* left), though no less appreciated by enthusiasts. It is made by boiling the head, tongue, neck, trimmings, and other leftovers from the pork-curing process for about twenty-four hours. The bones are then removed and the meat is cut into chunks and seasoned with salt, pepper, rosemary, garlic, and spices. The mixture is transferred into jute sacks, tied by hand, and left to dry for a day. *Soppressata* is eaten fresh, either sliced or cut into cubes.

SALSICCIA DI CINTA SENESE

Pork sausages are eaten three different ways in Florence: When fresh and soft, they are either spread raw on bread or they are grilled. When aged, they are sliced like salami. *Salsiccia di cinta senese* is made from the meat of an ancient breed of wild pig once prevalent in the Siennese countryside. *Cinta senese* pigs are easily recognizable by their black bodies and broad belt *(cinta)* of bristly white hair covering their upper backs and front legs. Their meat is dark, well marbled, and flavorful.

SBRICIOLONA

Sbriciolona is essentially a fresher version of *finocchiona*. It is recognizable by its size (it is larger in diameter than *finocchiona*) and even more so by its soft, crumbly texture—hence its name, *sbriciolona,* which means "crumbly." Wild fennel, with tall, feathery leaves and yellow flowers that yield the seeds used as a flavoring, grows throughout the countryside, which perhaps explains the popularity of fennel in many traditional Tuscan preparations.

When olives begin to turn from green to black on the trees, farmers test them for ripeness by picking a handful and rubbing them vigorously between their palms. If their hands smell like olive oil, the harvest begins.

TUSCAN OLIVE OIL

The Tuscan landscape is a patchwork of grapevines, cypress trees, farmhouses, and olive groves. The olive trees, with their gnarled trunks and silvery leaves, are studded each autumn with olives in shades from bright green to inky black.

The oil from these olives is the defining flavor of the Florentine kitchen—the smallest drizzling of it is enough to elevate the taste of anything it touches. Of course, it is rarely simply drizzled. Most people with a bit of storage room buy their oil for the whole year at harvesttime (calculating about a quart/liter a week for a family of four) and keep it in heavy glass tubs or stainless-steel containers to use as needed, which is often.

Salads are tossed with little more than olive oil and salt; bottled dressings are virtually unheard of. Cooked greens are dressed with olive oil and lemon. Cakes are made using olive oil instead of butter. *Il soffritto,* the sauté of onions, carrots, and celery that forms the base of so many recipes, begins with olive oil. Mothers give it to their babies, and *everyone* drenches toasted bread with it.

The truth is that Tuscans tend to be snobbish about their *olio* in a way they are about little else. They balk at oil from Spain, Greece, or even neighboring Liguria and shudder at the thought of the clear, bland, yellowish stuff peddled in supermarkets around the world as "extra-virgin olive oil."

The best Tuscan olive oils tend to be estate bottled, such as that from the Tenuta di Capezzana, where the olives are grown with the same meticulousness as the estate's wine grapes and are cold pressed at the estate's own *frantoio,* or olive mill. The "extra-virgin" moniker for this and other high-quality olive oils is a reference to acidity—or, rather, the lack thereof. Olives begin to become acidic soon after picking, so the faster they make it to the mill, the better the oil.

Olio nuovo, or just-pressed oil, is cause for celebration every November. The deep, murky green oil is richly fruity on the nose and tongue, with a wicked bite that catches at the back of the throat. After the oil has aged for a month or two, the bite mellows. Don't expect *olio nuovo* to be a bargain if you are lucky enough to get your hands on some, but pay happily, for it is well worth every cent.

In the city of Florence, some places to buy the best-quality olive oil are La Bottega della Frutta (on Via dei Federighi) and Zoccali Frutta e Verdura (on Via dei Neri). Or shop from vendors at both the San Lorenzo and the Sant'Ambrogio daily markets. Notable brands include Laudemio, Fattoria La Querce, and Fattoria il Poggio.

Most Tuscan olive pickers prefer to be paid in oil rather than cash.

The olive harvest excites Florentines like few other agricultural events. Though winemaking is integral to the ebb and flow of Tuscan seasons, it takes awhile, sometimes a very long while, for the fruit to make the journey from *uva* (grapes) to a drinkable *vino*. The olive harvest provides immediate gratification, since the oil is at its very best just after it is pressed.

Olive Varieties

Dozens of olive varieties are grown throughout the world, each with its own size, shape, flavor, and use in the kitchen. Tuscan olives are strictly about oil. The five primary varieties are *moraiolo* and *correggiolo* (the two predominant ones), *frantoio* (from the Italian word for olive mill), plump *leccino,* and *pendolino.* Capezzana, an estate-bottled Tuscan olive oil, is made from 60 percent *moraiolo* olives, 30 percent *frantoio,* 5 percent *leccino,* and 5 percent *pendolino* olives.

Authentic Tuscan Olive Oil

Choosing the best-quality Tuscan olive oil is not always easy, as the labels can be deceiving. A homey-looking bottle with an old-fashioned *casalinga* (housewife) holding an olive branch on its label might well be a low-grade, industrially made oil. A bottle labeled *olio di oliva toscano* could mean that the bottler purchased olives from as far away as Spain or Greece and then pressed them in an industrial mill somewhere in Tuscany. The problem with imported olives is twofold:

If they are not local varieties, they will differ in flavor from Tuscan olives. More importantly, because olives begin to oxidize soon after they are picked, those that have traveled are less fresh than locally picked olives. For truly authentic *olio extra vergine di oliva toscano*, look for artisan-made Tuscan oils. Their labels will show the year of harvest and confirm that the olives were grown on the estate and pressed at the estate's own *frantoio* or at a local nonindustrial mill.

Making Olive Oil

HARVESTING THE OLIVES Olives are harvested using large, long-handled wooden rakes. The freshly picked olives are then whisked off to the mill in crates to be pressed within thirty-six hours.

PRESSING THE OLIVES Traditionally, oil was extracted by pressing the olives between granite millstones. Many nonindustrial mills now use a modern continuous-cycle system. The olives are conveyed up a belt, washed, and cut into a pulp. The resulting paste is kneaded and centrifugally "decanted" to separate it into solids, water, and oil.

DISCARDING THE SANSA *Sansa* is the dirty, brown residue of oil production, consisting primarily of ground pits and skin. It is piled outside the mill to be picked up by refineries that use chemical solvents to extract additional but inferior oil.

COLLECTING THE OIL At the tail end of the enormous machinery used to extract oil is a spout from which pure oil flows in a thin stream. The oil is filtered and usually sent to an adjoining *orciaia* (olive oil storeroom) to rest in terra-cotta urns for several days before bottling.

In Florence drinking espresso is an essential daily habit. It is consumed at just about any time—for breakfast, as a midmorning or afternoon pick-me-up, or after meals, enjoyed plain, "stained" with milk, or "corrected" with a splash of liqueur.

CAFÉS

For many Florentines, mornings begin at what they refer to as *il bar,* or a café. Their café culture is not one of homey cooked breakfasts or leisurely brunches. The big meals are *pranzo* (lunch) and *cena* (dinner), with the *bar* serving for all those moments before and in between: breakfast, midmorning snack, early afternoon bite, and an *aperitivo* at the end of the day. The *bar*'s function seems to be as much social as gastronomic: It acts as a secular congregation place where life's events, from the grandest to the most mundane, are recounted, hashed out, loudly debated, or confided *sotto voce.*

Besides the coffee that is the mainstay of every *bar,* there is a row or two of bottles, including strange-seeming, unfamiliar items like Cynar (artichoke bitters), the brown, medicinal-tasting Fernet Branca (Italy's

favorite digestif), the ubiquitous rose red Campari, fiery grappa (page 51), and an assortment of other spirits, liqueurs, waters, and soft drinks. A glass case is filled with pastries both *dolci* (sweet), such as *budini di riso,* the delicious Florentine rice-custard breakfast puddings, and *salate* (savory), such as mozzarella and tomato sandwiches.

You might be surprised to find most patrons standing along the counter, sometimes two or three deep, eating and drinking *in piedi* rather than sitting down at a table and taking their time. Florence's café culture looks much more like a Formula One Ferrari refueling than an English high tea. Most cafés have at least a handful of tables; expect the swanky ones to have loads of them and to charge you handsomely for the privilege of taking your libation seated.

Such convivial places are legion in Florence, yet a handful stand out in the fray. For quality and location, it is hard to beat the grand Rivoire in Piazza della Signoria, makers of the city's best *cioccolata calda* (hot chocolate) as well as hand-wrapped chocolates made in the café's basement laboratory. Gilli, in Piazza della Repubblica, said to be the city's oldest café (it dates from 1789), is also one of the most beautiful, with Murano glass chandeliers and a sea of tables spilling out onto one of the city's busiest squares. Giacosa, on the elegant Via de' Tornabuoni, was once the city's most refined *bar.* Fashion designer Roberto Cavalli recently took over the location, retaining part of the shop for a "new" superchic Giacosa and adding to the *bar*'s traditional offerings new ones such as cakes and chocolates with Cavalli-inspired designs.

For an accomplished *barista*, espresso making is an art form.

Florentines measure the worth of a *bar* by its coffee—so much so that espresso machines are designed to hold an upended bag of roasted coffee beans in full display so that customers can see which roaster the *bar* uses. Italy grows no coffee beans itself, but imports them from Africa and South America and roasts them at home.

Roasting Coffee

Piansa is the city's premier coffee roaster, and owner Pietro Staderini approaches the task with the seriousness of an artisan. His blends are of the highest quality. He adds a superior robusta to first-class arabicas to round out the flavors and then roasts the beans in batches under 132 pounds (60 kg) for maximum control. The roasted beans must reach the deep brown of a monk's habit. Lighter beans, which indicate underripeness, are picked out by hand and discarded.

Il Barista

Every Florentine knows that it takes a good *barista* to make an espresso that is just the right *altezza* (height), with a thin layer of fine foam on top, and to heat, swirl, and pour the milk for a cappuccino so that it is hot but not scalding and neither overly milky nor foamy. Of course, these are only two of the most typical versions of *il caffè*. The number of standard coffee drinks and the specificity with which people order their daily brew are myriad. A *caffè* can be *macchiato* ("stained" with steamed milk), either *caldo* (hot) or *freddo* (cold). It can be *shakerato* (shaken with ice and sugar syrup), *doppio* (a double shot of espresso), *ristretto* (short), or *lungo* (long). A cappuccino can be *bollente* (scalding) or *tiepido* (lukewarm), *in tazza* (in a coffee cup) or *nel bicchiere* (in a glass), *con tanta schiuma* (foamy) or *poca schiuma* (milky). A good *barista* also remembers his or her customers' proclivities, knowing that for the most part they are creatures of habit.

Making the Ideal Espresso

GRINDING THE BEANS Coffee beans—much like spices—retain their flavor best when still whole. Most cafés grind their own beans in small batches to a very fine or medium-fine consistency. The best grinders are of the low-speed burr variety, which crush the beans uniformly between two cylinders without excessively heating them and thus altering their flavor.

TAMPING DOWN THE COFFEE After the coffee is released in calibrated doses from the grinder into the filter basket, it is tamped—flattened and compressed—so that all the coffee in the basket will be uniformly brewed. This is done with a handheld tamper rotated in a twisting motion.

PULLING THE SHOT The filter basket is secured in the espresso machine, and a demitasse cup is set under the spout. A push of a button or the pull of a handle "pulls" the shot, causing a thin stream of espresso to dribble out of the spout. Knowing when to retrieve the cup is an acquired skill. The inexperienced *barista* should allow between twenty and thirty seconds.

LATTE MACCHIATO

CAFFELLATTE

ESPRESSO

CAFFÈ LUNGO

ESPRESSO

This is the basic brew—the thick, flavorful liquid from which every variation is just that, a variation on the quintessential Italian coffee. The word *caffè*, without any qualifier, refers to an espresso. Espresso is served in a demitasse cup. Though the word conjures up the image of a tiny, delicate vessel, the reality is more often a thick, sturdy (albeit small) ceramic cup. A well-made espresso should be strong but not bitter and should be covered with a thin layer of pale, creamy foam.

CAFFELLATTE

Caffellatte, or *caffè latte,* is the universal coffee drink that everyone drank at home in the old days before the advent of modern espresso machines and the breakfast pit stop at the *bar.* It is still served in most traditional *pensioni* (inns) at breakfast time. *Caffellatte* is made by pouring roughly equal amounts of coffee (usually brewed in a stove-top *moka,* or coffeemaker) and hot milk from two separate pitchers into a large coffee cup or bowl.

CAFFÈ LUNGO

A *caffè lungo* is a "long" coffee, made so by letting an extra amount of hot water pass through the espresso grounds. It should not be confused with a *caffè americano,* which is essentially an espresso *allungato* (lengthened) by adding hot water to a pulled espresso. While this drink has its fans, many real coffee lovers find the *caffè lungo* too bitter (since bitterness comes out of the ground beans with longer brewing) and the *caffè americano* too watered down.

LATTE MACCHIATO

More or less the opposite of a *caffè macchiato* (see right), a *latte macchiato* is milk "stained" with coffee to a delicate, pale tan. *Latte macchiato* is generally served in a moderately tall glass rather than a coffee cup. The milk is steamed until hot, but not frothy. Then a shot of espresso is poured into the glass. The result is a warming, milky drink with a gentle hint of the coffee's rich flavor.

CAFFÈ MAROCCHINO

CAPPUCCINO

CAFFÈ MACCHIATO

CAFFÈ CORRETTO

CAFFÈ MACCHIATO

Macchiare means "to stain" in Italian, and a *caffè macchiato* is "stained" with milk—that is, with just a dollop of frothy steamed milk on top of the espresso. A *caffè macchiato* can be *freddo* (cold) or *caldo* (hot). While tradition frowns upon a postprandial cappuccino, there is no similar proscription to adding a touch of milk to an espresso after a meal. Note that *macchiati* are garnished with milk rather than cream.

CAPPUCCINO

Also known in Florence by its nickname, *cappuccio*, this most favorite of all espresso-and-milk combinations purportedly got its name from its resemblance in color to the robes of Capuchin monks. A *barista* generally begins steaming the milk before pulling the shot. The milk should neither be allowed to heat to scalding nor left to separate into hot milk and dry froth. The latter is avoided by tapping the pitcher against the counter and pouring the milk with a particular shaking motion known mainly to the experienced *barista*.

CAFFÈ CORRETTO

This drink, an espresso "corrected" with a splash of spirits, is surprisingly popular first thing in the morning, especially on cold winter days. It is not enough to simply order a *caffè corretto;* you need to let the *barista* know what to correct it *with*. The options are many: grappa—a dry, colorless brandy distilled from grape pomace—is a favorite, but other choices include whiskey, brandy, Sambuca (an Italian anise-flavored liqueur), or Fernet Branca (a bitter, brown Italian *digestivo,* or digestive liqueur, made from a mixture of nearly forty herbs).

CAFFÈ MAROCCHINO

A *caffè marocchino* is immediately recognizable by its short glass cup with a thin metal base and handle. It is made by sprinkling an espresso with cocoa powder and topping the whole with a dollop of steamed milk. While some sprinkle the cocoa over the top, others put a dash of cocoa into the glass before the coffee. Still others dust both before and after. The origins of the name *marocchino*, which means "Moroccan coffee," are unknown. In Morocco, coffee is a thick, highly sweetened brew.

Chianti became one of the world's first officially designated wine production areas in 1716, when Grand Duke Cosimo III de' Medici laid down a decree defining the region's boundaries and setting forth a series of rules for its wine production.

TUSCAN WINE

For centuries, Tuscany's archetypal wine was Chianti, made in the region of the same name that begins just south of Florence and continues almost as far as Siena. In pre-industrialized Italy, it was a thirst quencher, sold *sfuso* (unbottled) or in the straw-covered *fiaschi* synonymous with checkered tablecloths and cheap Italian eateries. Later it was mass-produced, with quantity taking precedence over quality—but no longer. In the last few decades, Chianti has undergone a renaissance in winemaking, and the area now produces some of the most exciting wines in Italy.

Sangiovese (blood of Jupiter) is the Tuscan wine grape *per eccellenza,* yielding slightly acidic, earthy wines, low in fruit and tannins. Tuscan winemakers consider the Sangiovese grape to be one of the great patrimonies of their *territorio.* This concept, analogous to

the French notion of *terroir,* relates to the characteristics of both the soil and weather and their effects on the flavor of the wine. Sangiovese grapes require terrain with low humidity, southern exposure, and rocky, friable soil that drains well. It is the predominant grape in Chianti, and historically was blended with Canaiolo and white Trebbiano and Malvasia grapes.

In the 1960s, the Italian government introduced a system of rules to regulate wine production known as DOC *(Denominazione di Origine Controllata)* and DOCG *(Denominazione di Origine Controllata e Garantita).* To carry the DOC or the even more stringent DOCG label, a wine must be produced in a particular geographical area, contain a certain percentage of prescribed grape varietals, and follow specific standards for aging, among other

rules. Though such regulations aim at ensuring quality, they left little room for winemakers to develop nontraditional techniques.

New governmental regulations permit Chianti wines to contain up to 20 percent of international varieties such as Merlot, Cabernet Sauvignon, and Syrah. These changes, as well as new planting and aging practices adopted by such wineries as Castello di Fonterutoli, Isole e Olena, Castello di Brolio, and Fontodi, are producing well-structured, deeply hued, fruitier wines that hold up well in the cellar.

A parallel development in the Tuscan wine world was the advent of the so-called Super Tuscans. Born in the wild seaside hills of the Maremma southwest of Florence, particularly the Bolgheri area, Super Tuscans are credited in great part to the Antinori family, Florentine winemakers since the fourteenth century.

Florentines cannot imagine a fine meal unaccompanied by a glass of wine.

Super Tuscan is not an appellation but rather a colloquial reference that originally referred to wines that fell outside the DOC and DOCG governmental standards, but that were worthy of a title nonetheless. Now, many Super Tuscans carry more recently created classifications, most notably IGT *(Indicazione Geografica Tipica)*. Typically, a Super Tuscan contains international grape varietals such as Cabernet Sauvignon or Merlot and is aged in *barriques* (small French oak barrels).

Antinori's Tignanello, the first Super Tuscan to blend Sangiovese with a certain percentage of Cabernet Sauvignon, has met with resounding acclaim, as have the

casks of oak or chestnut. *Vin santo* of this quality is known as a *vino da meditazione,* no longer merely a dessert wine but one worthy of being savored all on its own.

When in Florence, take a drive out to the countryside to visit a winery or two. Fontodi, nestled in the heart of the Chianti Classico wine region, exemplifies much of what is best about Tuscan winemaking today. Its newly constructed cellar is outfitted with the most sophisticated vinification equipment available, which operates ingeniously on purely gravitational principles. The Capezzana cellar is ancient and full of history (the cellar was partially walled up during World War II to

Super Tuscans were wines of such superb quality that to label them simply *vino da tavola* (table wine) seemed like heresy.

winery's Solaia (a Cabernet base blended with Sangiovese) and the wines of its Ornellaia estate. Other first-class wineries, such as Fattoria Le Pupille and Jacopo Banti, have followed suit with innovative Super Tuscan blends of their own.

To the west of Florence is the wine area of Carmignano, dominated by the Capezzana winery, whose Villa di Capezzana and Ghiaie della Furba wines have earned top honors in the respected Gambero Rosso guide to Italian wines. To the east of Florence is the Rufina area, where the Marchesi de' Frescobaldi, noble Florentine winemakers, produce their outstanding Chianti Rufina Montesodi. Siena's hilltowns are home to the lofty Brunello di Montalcino wines and the more affordable Vino Nobile di Montepulciano.

The best Tuscan wineries almost always make a *vin santo,* the sweet amber dessert wine that marks the end of many a Florentine meal. The process for making *vin santo* is long and arduous—white grapes, usually Malvasia, are air-dried on rush mats for months, then pressed and vinified for three years in small

hide precious bottles from occupying forces). The Rufina area's Fattoria Selvapiana, with its seventeenth-century villa, formal gardens, and good-natured willingness to educate its visitors, is also worthy of a visit.

If you are unable to visit a winery, stop by one of Florence's excellent wine shops instead. Le Volpi e l'Uva (near the Palazzo Pitti) and Fuori Porta (near Porta San Niccolò) are two of the best. The charming Boccadama in Piazza Santa Croce has a thoughtful selection of Italian and international wines, as well as a restaurant with outdoor seating in one of the city's most beautiful squares. Another worthy stop is the Enoteca Fratelli Zanobini on Via Sant'Antonino near the San Lorenzo market, where you can take your glass into the bustling market street or buy bottles to take away. For yet another (literally) pedestrian experience, head to the lively Via dei Neri and visit All'Antico Vinaio, or another one of Florence's few remaining *fiaschetterie*— appealingly atmospheric, unpretentious wine bars selling *vino sfuso* (unbottled wine) and *stuzzichini* (snacks).

The ancient Etruscans—the most powerful civilization in pre-Roman Italy—were already making wine in what is now Tuscany in 900 BC. They poured their *vino* into clay flasks known as *oinochoe.* Over the millennia, Tuscan winemaking has evolved into a fascinating blend of agriculture and technology, producing wines that have won the region worldwide acclaim.

The Harvest

Every year, sometime between late summer and early autumn, the Tuscan *vendemmia,* or grape harvest, begins. The grapes grow best when the summer is long and hot, the breezes gentle, and the rain occasional but not too close to harvesttime. Even the best-kept vineyards are prey to the whims of nature—a freak summer *grandinata* (hailstorm) can ruin an entire harvest. Most years are blessedly lacking in drama, and the ripe bunches are picked, as always, by hand.

Barrel Aging

The wine cellar feels as quiet as a tomb after all the activity in the vineyard, with its legions of pickers and noisy tractors, and the hum of machinery in the winery as the grapes are stemmed and crushed. By comparison, the cellar may simply look like a room full of wooden barrels because its real activity takes place slowly, over time, within the quiet darkness of the *botte* (barrel).

Though it is axiomatic among wine lovers that fermentation and aging can only enhance the essential qualities of the fruit itself, proper aging can make the difference between a fine wine and an extraordinary one. Aging wines in *botti di legno* (small barrels also known by their French name, *barriques*) matures them so that they become smooth and complex. Oak is the wood of choice because its composition and porosity impart flavor and tannins better than other woods. The duration of barrel aging depends on the wine, the winemaker, and the age and size of the barrels. Some barrel-aged Tuscan reds spend only three to six months in wood, while a Brunello di Montalcino spends a minimum of four years.

The Winemaking Process

PICKING GRAPES At many of Tuscany's premier wineries, only expert pickers make the first round of the vineyards, harvesting ripe bunches and leaving the rest to be picked days later when they reach their full sweet and juicy maturity.

DESTEMMING AND CRUSHING Tractors cart the *uva* (grapes) to the winery, where they are loaded into a large metal hopper. The hopper tips the grapes into a destemming machine that feeds the cleaned grapes into a closed chamber, where they are crushed into juice.

FERMENTATION The *mosto* (must, or grape juice) is pumped into stainless-steel vats or wooden barrels to ferment. Over time, the pulp, skins, and seeds of red wine grapes rise to the top and must be pushed back into the juice, lest they oxidize.

OXYGENATION The new wine will be best if it is oxygenated after fermentation. Wine in a stainless-steel vat is allowed to gush out into an open container, where it froths in the air before being transferred to a new vat. Wooden barrels are porous, so oxygenation happens naturally.

VERMENTINO DI
BOLGHERI

VERNACCIA DI SAN
GIMIGNANO

CHIANTI

VINO ROSATO

CHIANTI CLASSICO
RISERVA

VERNACCIA DI SAN GIMIGNANO

Tuscany's best-known white wine, made in the area surrounding the medieval hilltown of San Gimignano, has the distinction of being the first wine granted DOC *(Denominazione di Origine Controllata)* status in 1966. (It now carries the even more stringently regulated DOCG status *(Denomi- nazione di Origine Controllata e Garantita)*. While traditional Vernaccia wines tend to be full- bodied, the current trend leans toward making the wines lighter and crisper.

VERMENTINO DI BOLGHERI

The town of Bolgheri and its surrounding countryside along the *Costa degli Etruschi* (Etruscan coast) is home to the celebrated Ornellaia and Sassicaia wines, as well as Vermentino di Bolgheri, a crisp, citrusy wine made from a grape of the same name.

VINO ROSATO

Vino rosato is a treat in Tuscany, where rosé wine is not as common as it is in places like the south of France. It is generally made with red wine grapes whose dark skins are left only very briefly to ferment with the grape juice.

CHIANTI

Chianti is the wine once synony- mous with Tuscan winemaking, if not the whole of Italian wine. Chianti Classico, from the well- demarcated geographic region between Siena and the hills south of Florence, is characterized by a ruby red color and hints of black cherry. It is denoted by the symbol of a black rooster—*gallo nero*— while Chianti from other Tuscan areas is called Chianti Putto (*putto* means "cherub"). It is often served in liter, half-liter, or even quarter- liter carafes or poured into short glass tumblers.

CHIANTI CLASSICO RISERVA

Riserva (reserve) is a label that can be appended only to Italian wines classified under the DOC or DOCG system. Not only are these wines aged longer than other traditional vintages of their category—in this case Chianti Classico—but in most instances only a winery's very best wines are selected to become *riserve*. Chianti Classico Riserva is aged for more than two years, at least one of which is usually an *affinamento* (aging and refinement) in small oak *barriques*. These wines tend to be richer and can be held longer than regular Chianti Classico.

VINO NOBILE DI
MONTEPULCIANO

BRUNELLO DI
MONTALCINO

SUPER TUSCAN

GRAPPA

VIN SANTO

VINO NOBILE DI MONTEPULCIANO

Montepulciano is Tuscany's highest hilltown. The town is famous for its beautiful buildings and churches, and the surrounding hills for the "noble" wine that they produce—so-called because it had once been known as the "king" of wines. The dominant grape in Vino Nobile di Montepulciano is Prugnolo, the name for local Sangiovese, which is blended with red Canaiolo grapes and a small percentage of other varieties. The wine is aged for two to three years in oak or chestnut barrels and has pronounced Bing cherry qualities.

BRUNELLO DI MONTALCINO

Reputed to be Tuscany's greatest wine, on par with the Barolo wines of Piedmont, Brunello is named after both the town of Montalcino, in whose hills it is made, and the Sangiovese grape clone Brunello, a strain of Sangiovese Grosso with deep brown skin. Regular Brunello is aged for at least four years, while Brunello Riserva must be aged for five years. In both cases, the aging process gives the wine a rich, deep color and powerful structure. It is best served in a wineglass with a deep, wide bowl to capture the wine's bouquet.

SUPER TUSCAN

The advent of the Super Tuscan occurred less than three decades ago. Tenuta San Guido's Sassicaia (a Cabernet Sauvignon–Cabernet Franc blend) was the first. The name originally referred to a category of wines made outside the DOC and DOCG systems. Such wines would have been considered simply *vini da tavola* (table wines) in the past, but today they have a standardized system of their own, known as IGT (*Indicazione Geografica Tipica*). Super Tuscans, modeled after the great wines of Bordeaux, are of such depth that their title is well deserved.

GRAPPA

Grappa, a fiery, translucent spirit, is made by distilling the grape skins and seeds left over from the winemaking process. It is most commonly produced in northern Italy, but Tuscan winemakers have begun making it as well.

VIN SANTO

Vin santo, or "holy wine," is made from semidried white grapes that are pressed and then aged in small oak or chestnut casks. Storing the wine for years in rooms with widely fluctuating temperatures helps give it a deep amber color and caramel-like flavor.

Country houses of old were equipped with a wood-burning oven as well as a *madia,* a rectangular wooden chest with a hinged cover. Bread dough was kneaded on the *madia,* and flour, yeast, and heavy golden loaves of baked bread were stored inside.

ARTISAN BREAD

You might be surprised to learn Florentines are not nearly as particular about pasta as they are about bread. Theirs is not a slender baguette, but a fat, oval loaf often weighing more than two pounds (1 kg). A typical *pane toscano* has a thick golden crust, a moist and chewy crumb, and a flavor Tuscans affectionately describe as *sciocco*—insipid. Why? Because it is the humblest version of one of the most basic foods, entirely saltless, made solely from flour, water, and a knob of yesterday's leavened dough.

The history behind the bread-making tradition is an investigation into the Florentine psyche. In the days before unification, when Italy was a collection of querulous city-states, Florence got its salt from the neighboring maritime republic of Pisa. As the story goes, Florentines grew so tired of finding the Pisan

gabelliere at the door to collect the salt tax that they not only coined the adage "meglio un morto in casa che un pisano alla porta" (better a dead man in the house than a Pisan at the door) but also—in typical hardheaded Florentine fashion—decided to retaliate by making their bread without salt.

Whether *pane sciocco* survived the ages because Florentine staples like *prosciutto crudo* (salt-cured pork) were already so well suited for saltless bread, or because Florentine cuisine, which tends toward saltiness, adapted itself to the bread, is up for debate. The fact remains that over the centuries necessity evolved into tradition. *Pane sciocco* not only is the bread of choice for most Florentines, but also, because of its aging qualities, it has become an indispensable ingredient in *panzanella* (page 105), *pappa al pomodoro*

(page 110), and *ribollita* (page 118), three of the city's most beloved dishes.

Schiacciata, the ubiquitous Florentine flatbread—dimpled, scattered with salt, and doused with local olive oil—is made from the same saltless dough as *pane toscano.* Some bakers also make a crisp, paper-thin *schiacciata* that resembles the Sardinian specialty, *carta da musica* (sheet music).

The *panificio* (bread store) Salvadori in the Mercato di Sant'Ambrogio has an impressive selection of traditional Tuscan as well as organic and herbed breads. La Raccolta, a health-food store on Via Leopardi, sells Forno La Torre's wonderful organic Tuscan bread. Antica Dolce Forneria, in the town of San Casciano, makes exceptional breads, as does the Forno di Stefano Galli, with several locations throughout Florence.

Every bakery in Florence makes at least one version of *schiacciata*, if not several—thick, thin, or crackerlike, or scattered with a variety of toppings. The glass display case of every *bar* and café is sure to have a selection of *schiacciata* sandwiches filled with anything from thin slices of prosciutto or mozzarella and tomato to layers of tuna, lettuce, and mayonnaise.

Schiacciata Variations

Schiacciata at its most basic is simply brushed with olive oil and sprinkled with salt before baking and can be used as a sandwich bread. Or the unbaked dough can be dressed up in a variety of ways. *Rosmarino* (rosemary) has always been a favorite topping. Other toppings include thinly sliced onions, tomatoes, or zucchini (courgettes). Brushing the *schiacciata* dough with tomato paste slightly diluted with water gives the baked bread a beautiful russet color.

Yeast Starter

La madre (mother), as it is affectionately called, is the yeast starter, without which neither Tuscan bread nor *schiacciata* could reach such dizzying levels of deliciousness. Yeast is a microscopic organism that, when fed a mixture of flour and water, produces the carbon dioxide responsible for making bread rise. Modern industrial bread baking throughout most of the world uses commercial yeasts (either in packets of dried granules or in moist cakes of compressed fresh yeast).

The best Florentine bakers eschew commercial yeast in favor of their own wild yeast starter called *la biga*. Theirs is a world where bread making still has the mystery and delight of alchemy. Yeast starters are usually set in motion by "captured" wild airborne yeasts combined with water and flour; the mixture ferments and bubbles once the yeast is activated. When the mixture is regularly fed additional flour and water for a period of time, it is ready to use for bread making. Part of the starter goes into the bread, and part is reserved (and regularly fed) to perpetuate the starter batch for subsequent baking.

Making Schiacciata

KNEADING Flour, water, salt, and yeast starter (the exact proportions vary among bakers) are mixed together in a bowl. When the mixture forms a sticky mass, it is turned onto a work surface to be kneaded. This helps the gluten in wheat flour form into pliable strands that trap the carbon dioxide from the yeast and cause the bread to rise.

RISING The dough is subject to two rising periods, the first about four hours (after which the dough is punched down), the second about two. This process cannot be rushed.

SHAPING After the dough has risen a second time, it is formed into a large rectangle and placed on a floured baking sheet, then is dimpled by the baker, giving *schiacciata* its uneven surface.

BAKING *Schiacciata,* as its name (which translates as "flattened" or "squashed") attests, is a thin bread with a correspondingly shorter baking time than that of most loaf breads. The scent of the toasting flour on the bottom of the *schiacciata* is usually enough to tell a baker when the bread is ready to be removed from the oven.

The impulse to pair aged pecorino cheese with fig jam, quince paste, or chestnut honey, popular among cheese aficionados worldwide, is said to have been born in 1719 during a banquet celebrating *carnevale* in the Tuscan town of Siena.

ARTISAN CHEESE

Once the Tuscan countryside was filled with small family farms. Each had an ox for working the land; chickens, rabbits, and pigs for eating; and goats and sheep for milk. Tuscany's demographics have changed enormously over the past fifty years, with farmers migrating to the cities and city folk taking to the countryside for the sheer pleasure of living there. But like so many Tuscan culinary traditions forged in the past, sheep's milk cheese, or pecorino (from the word *pecora* for "sheep"), has remained Tuscany's most characteristic cheese and the one for which it is justifiably renowned.

Not to be confused with *pecorino romano,* which is a dry, hard grating cheese from Lazio, or the salty, piquant *pecorino sardo* from the island of Sardinia, *pecorino toscano* embodies an entire world of cheese making.

In the spring, when the sheep graze on fragrant wild grasses, cheese makers produce *marzolino,* a soft, fresh, mildly tart pecorino cheese. Other pecorino cheeses are *stagionato* (aged) to various degrees, from forty days (still a relatively fresh cheese) to up to ten months or more. Younger cheeses usually have pale, straw-colored rinds and a semisoft milky interior. Aged cheeses have dark orange rinds (or even black rinds if they have been coated in ash) and a sharp piquant flavor, and though they are quite firm, they are never hard enough to be grated.

As with most things Italian, nothing is wasted in the cheese-making process. From the curds comes the cheese, and from the whey comes an incredibly delicate, light ricotta that can be eaten fresh with olive oil, salt, and pepper, or used in *primi* (such as

ravioli stuffed with ricotta and spinach) and *dolci* (like the delicate *torta di ricotta*).

The southern Tuscan town of Pienza and its surrounding hillsides are synonymous with pecorino cheese. One of the area's producers, Caseificio Crete Senesi, makes a variety of excellent pecorinos, many of which are preserved in oil or are flavored with herbs and spices. In Sovicille, near Siena, the Azienda Agricola Cavazzoni makes wonderful organic pecorino cheese, and south of Florence, in the lush hills of San Pancrazio, the family-owned Fattoria Corzano e Paterno produces some of the region's finest pecorino.

Within Florence, Nello Formaggi, inside the Mercato di Sant'Ambrogio; Quercioli & Palli, on Via dei Neri; and La Bottega della Frutta, on Via dei Federighi, are fine places to buy pecorino cheese.

Fresh ricotta is one of the first foods a Florentine mother feeds her baby.

The best *pecorino artigianale* (artisan-made pecorino) comes from the milk of a cheese maker's own herds, which can number anywhere from two hundred to more than six hundred sheep. The animals are allowed to graze freely on pastures covered with alfalfa and fragrant wild grasses and are milked daily, except during the heat of the summer, when they stop producing milk.

The Rind

The *buccia,* or rind, of a pecorino cheese can be very revealing. The rind darkens as the cheese ages. Fresh *pecorino marzolino* has no rind at all. A *pecorino semi stagionato* (aged for only a short time) has a pale rind. Some cheeses are coated with tomato paste, giving the rinds an orange hue; others with ash, giving them dark gray rinds. Certain specialty pecorinos are covered in a milky white *muffa nobile* ("noble," or edible, mold), and others with walnut leaves.

Flavor Variations

Flavoring pecorino with herbs and spices is a relatively new trend. Traditionalists tend to look diffidently upon flavored cheeses. In their opinion, any herb flavor that a pecorino possesses should come from the grasses on which the sheep feed, not from flavorings, however "natural," added to the cheese. This may be true—to a point. A low-grade industrial cheese maker may try to enhance the taste of an otherwise uninteresting cheese with flakes of *peperoncino* (chile) or dried porcino mushrooms. Yet to dismiss the whole category of flavored cheeses is to paint with too broad a brush.

Some of Tuscany's most innovative cheese makers are experimenting by blending mixed herbs such as tarragon, rosemary, sage, and juniper into the curds before the cheeses are transferred to molds and allowed to set. The results are intriguing and delicious. Other pleasing pecorino cheeses called *pecorini tartufati* are enhanced with highly aromatic black or white truffles. Additional flavorings include arugula (rocket), garlic, parsley, olives, peppercorns, and even saffron.

Making Fresh Pecorino

BREAKING APART THE CURDS First fresh sheep's milk is heated to about 144°F (62°C). After cooling, it is reheated to about 92°F (33°C). Rennet, a coagulating enzyme, is added to the hot milk, causing it to separate into curds and whey. A long-handled metal rake or spiral whisk is pulled through the curds, breaking them into squares.

TRANSFERRING THE CURDS INTO MOLDS Depending on the particular pecorino cheese being made, the curds are either scooped or ladled into individual, usually round, molds.

SALTING The filled molds are placed in a steam oven heated to 95°F (35°C), where they remain for three to four hours while the curds settle. The cheese is then cured by rubbing its surface with salt or by submerging it in a *salamoia* (salt brine) for about twenty-four hours.

AGING After salt curing, the cheese is sent to a ventilated aging room. It is turned frequently during the aging period, which can last from three to nine months. Some cheeses are rubbed with olive oil to keep their rinds moist and free of mold.

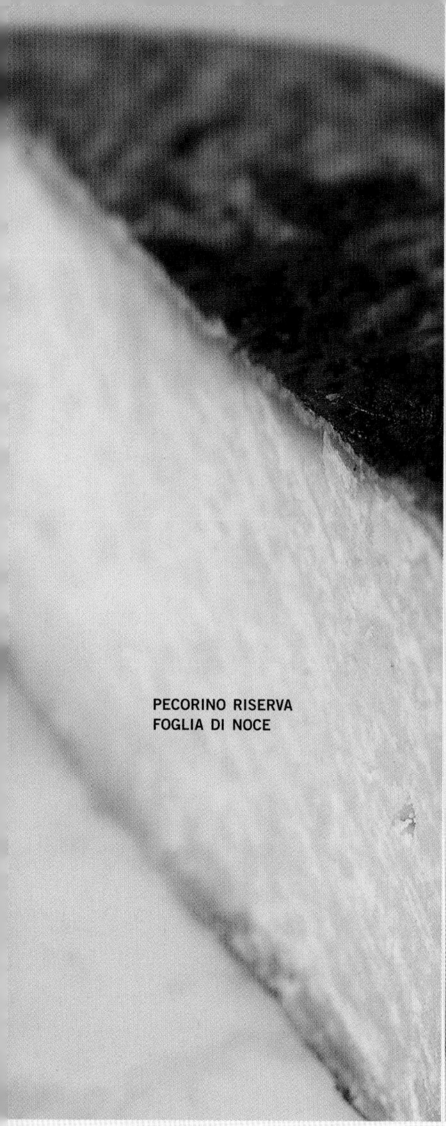

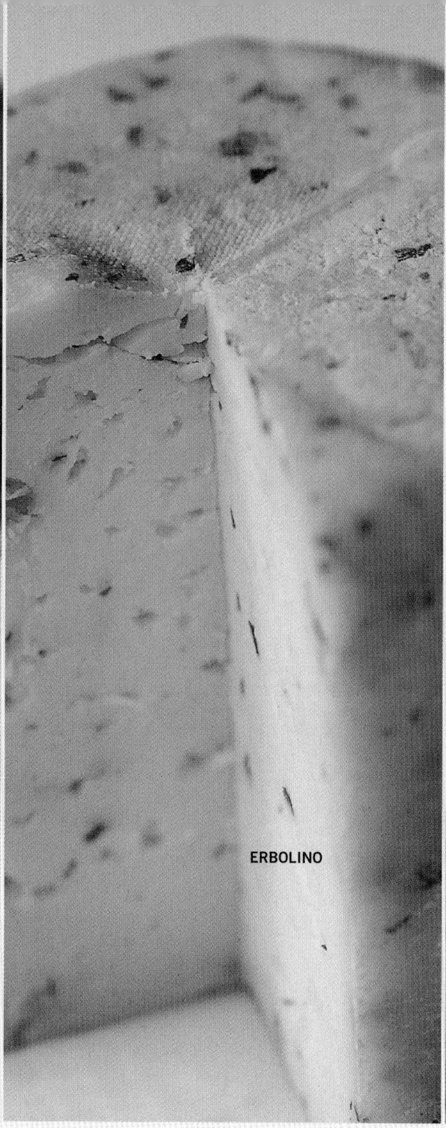

PECORINO RISERVA
FOGLIA DI NOCE

ERBOLINO

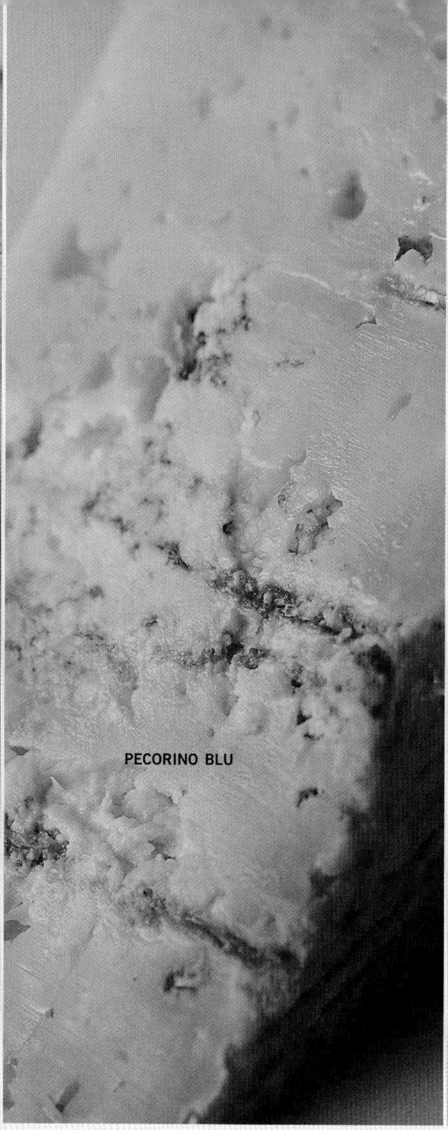

PECORINO BLU

PECORINO DI FOSSA

PECORINO RISERVA FOGLIA DI NOCE

Cheese makers refer to pecorino aged under walnut leaves as being *fermentato,* or fermented. This version is made by placing a three-month-old pecorino in an old wine barrel, surrounding it with walnut leaves, and allowing it to age for at least another forty days. The characteristically piquant cheese is easy to spot at the market since a few withered, black walnut leaves are usually still pressed onto the surface of the dark rind. Expect it to be more costly than a traditionally made pecorino.

ERBOLINO

One of the many up-and-coming varieties of herbed, fresh pecorino, *erbolino* is flavored with garlic, red pepper flakes, parsley, and rosemary. Soft herbed cheeses are best in the springtime, when the sheep feed on abundant spring grasses and produce large quantities of flavorful milk. *Erbolino* makes a good *stuzzichino* (snack), cut into cubes and eaten alone or sliced into thin wedges and served with crisp, crackerlike *schiacciata.*

PECORINO BLU

Blue cheeses are made by exposing cheeses to molds that form blue or green veins throughout, giving them an intense flavor and scent. Gorgonzola, from the town of the same name near Milan, is Italy's most famous Italian *blu.* Fattoria Corzano e Paterno's *pecorino blu* is made by curdling sheep's milk in a particular way, then adding to it the same penicillin culture that is used to make Gorgonzola. The result is an unusual, elegant dessert cheese.

PECORINO DI FOSSA

This cheese is currently Tuscany's most hyped pecorino, the making of which is mysterious enough to pique the interest of even the most skeptical. During August, rounds of specially selected three- to four-month-old pecorino cheese are wrapped in white cotton and buried in deep earthen *fosse* (pits) whose walls have been covered with hay, straw, and various wild grasses. The pit is then sealed for one hundred days. When the pit is opened, the cotton cloth has become covered with a fine mold, and the cheese that emerges is spicy and pungent.

PECORINO STAGIONATO

PECORINO GRAN RISERVA

BUCCIA DI ROSPO

PECORINO FRESCO DOLCE

PECORINO STAGIONATO

Just how *stagionato* (aged) an aged pecorino will be depends on the *caseificio* (cheese dairy). Typically, a *pecorino stagionato* spends about nine months in the cheese cellar, during which time each cheese is turned periodically and may be rubbed with *la morchia* (olive oil dregs) and covered in *cenere* (ash). Ash is said to help draw humidity out of the cheese, so that once it is fully aged, its consistency will allow the cheese to be cut easily into thin shavings.

PECORINO GRAN RISERVA

This artisan cheese maker's premier aged pecorino may spend up to eighteen months in the cheese cellar before being sent to market. The structure of this cheese causes it to cut rather unevenly, not unlike Parmigiano-Reggiano, which is aged for even longer. A glass of full-bodied red wine and a wedge of well-aged *pecorino gran riserva* accompanied by a bit of chestnut honey, quince paste, or fig jam make a lovely end to an elegant Tuscan meal.

BUCCIA DI ROSPO

Only one cheese maker, Fattoria Corzano e Paterno, makes this cheese, poetically named *buccia di rospo* (toad's skin) for its warty surface. Like many gastronomic delicacies, it was born of error—in this case when excess humidity in the cheese cellar caused a pecorino to ferment under its rind. The resulting cheese is creamier than most pecorinos and has a slightly acrid odor and full flavor. *Buccia di rospo* has been compared with the sharp, buttery Taleggio of Lombardy.

PECORINO FRESCO DOLCE

After *marzolino* (the super-fresh, soft cheese made in spring with sheep's milk), *pecorino fresco* is the least aged of all pecorino cheeses. It has a pale, smooth rind, a creamy interior, and a delicate, nutty flavor that Florentines refer to as *dolce,* which translates as "sweet," but in this context means only lightly salted. As pecorino ages, it becomes more *saporito,* literally "flavorful," though in Tuscany the word denotes a pleasant saltiness.

First-time visitors to Florence have been known to make a habit of stopping for gelato, punctuating the space between every meal with *un cono* or *una coppa* of their favorite flavors, twisting their tongues around words like *gianduia* (chocolate and hazelnut) and *stracciatella* (chocolate chip).

GELATO

The origins of gelato are somewhat contested, but most people attribute the first modern technique for freezing egg custard, sugar, and flavorings to the Florentine genius Bernardo Buontalenti—Renaissance poet, sculptor, painter, and inventor. The technique was perfected in Paris by Sicilian Francesco Procopio dei Coltelli, whose famous café Le Procope is still going strong today.

Gelato is big business in modern Italy. In October 2003, Florence hosted the International Handmade Gelato fair, which included seminars on such topics as "Gelato in the Diets of People of All Ages." As the fair's title indicates, the best gelati are *artigianali* (artisan made), the operative syllable being *art*. This edible art is created from fresh, authentic ingredients—cream, milk, and eggs, as well as pistachios, pine nuts, bittersweet chocolate, or anything else that tickles the taste buds of the *gelataio*. No stabilizers, thickeners, or emulsifiers are used. Gelato's texture comes from the softness created by tiny air bubbles trapped in the emulsion and the creaminess of the various fats (milk, eggs, and flavorings such as nuts and chocolate) dispersed among the ice crystals. *Gelaterie* also offer bright, refreshing *sorbetti,* which are water- rather than cream-based and have flavors as varied as the fruits of the earth. The best part of the gelato experience is that one can be greedy without being gluttonous: even the smallest cup or cone can be made up of three flavors, and the larger ones can include as many as five.

The Vivoli family has been making gelato at the same small shop near the Santa Croce church for more than seventy years. From the moment its doors open in the morning, tourists flock there (locals show up at more customary hours), as intent on eating the famed gelato as they are on seeing Michelangelo's *David* or the Uffizi Gallery.

The tiny *latteria* (dairy) on Via San Miniato near the Porta San Niccolò makes light and milky gelati, as well as *semifreddi* (literally, "half cold"), a type of soft, rich ice cream, much like a frozen mousse. Carabé on Via Ricasoli is renowned for its Sicilian gelati and *granite* (granitas), the slushy frozen drinks popular in southern Italy. The Gelateria dei Neri (on Via dei Neri) also makes excellent gelati. Outside the city, in the main square of the town of Impruneta, Bar Italia offers gelato so wonderful that city dwellers take a Sunday drive to the country just for the pleasure of a cup or cone.

Florentines generally do not eat in the streets, but gelato is an exception.

SORBETTO DI FRAGOLA

SORBETTO DI LIMONE

GELATO DI NOCCIOLA

GELATO DI STRACCIATELLA

SORBETTO DI FRAGOLA

Italians wouldn't dream of eating North America's anemically pastel-colored strawberry ice cream if they could have a bright pinkish red *sorbetto di fragola* (strawberry sorbet) instead. In Italy fruits are usually—though not always—fashioned into *sorbetti* rather than gelati. *Fragola* tends to be a *gelateria* standard and is always found in late spring when the fruits are at their prime.

SORBETTO DI LIMONE

Light, tart, and refreshing, this is the flavor for the days when the fair city of Florence is so swelteringly hot that its cobblestones seem to sizzle and a gelato break is the only way to survive the unrelenting heat. *Limone* is also the flavor of choice on rare formal occasions when *sorbetto* is served to cleanse the palate between courses. It is delicious paired with a more substantial gelato like chocolate.

GELATO DI NOCCIOLA

Nocciola, or hazelnut (filbert), is one of Tuscany's favorite nuts. Hazel trees, with their bright green leaves and abundance of small, round nuts covered in leafy casings, are common in the Tuscan countryside. The nuts, often toasted, are more commonly used in ice creams and baked desserts than eaten out of hand. Hazelnuts define *gelato di nocciola,* but also find their way into other flavors, such as *gelato di gianduia,* which gets its name from the chocolate and hazelnut cream-filled candies called *gianduiotti*.

GELATO DI STRACCIATELLA

As beloved in Florence as it is throughout North America, *gelato di stracciatella* (chocolate chip) purportedly got its name from the Roman egg-drop chicken soup of the same name. The bits of chocolate, which tend to look more like tiny shavings than actual chips, are said to resemble the egg threads in the soup.

GELATO DI CIOCCOLATO

GELATO DI CREMA

GELATO DI PISTACCHIO

GELATO DI FIOR DI LATTE

GELATO DI CIOCCOLATO

The *gusto* (flavor) chocolate fans inevitably head for first, *cioccolato* is generally of the deep, dark variety—*fondente,* as it is called in Italy. Some *gelaterie* scatter tiny flecks of dark chocolate over the tub of freshly made *gelato al cioccolato.* A popular chocolate-based flavor is *bacio* (kisses). It is named after—and made with—Baci Perugini, a brand of foil-wrapped chocolate and hazel-nut bonbons, each containing a slip of paper with a romantic quote or bit of poetry.

GELATO DI CREMA

This gelato is surprisingly eggy for those expecting its vanilla color to yield a vanilla ice-cream taste. The intense flavor, however, is exactly what aficionados want when they order what is essentially egg-custard ice cream. Artisan-made *crema* has a delicate creaminess that attests to the high quality of Tuscan eggs. Since the flavor of *gelato di crema* relies so heavily on eggs, it is at its very best when its primary ingredient is both farm fresh and organic.

GELATO DI PISTACCHIO

Pistachios tend to be associated more with the cuisines of the Middle East than with Italy, where they are also cultivated. Sicily makes frequent culinary uses of *pistacchi,* and they are occasional ingredients in savory fillings or stuffings in other parts of Italy. But in Florence, the pale green nuts are usually found still in their shells on the counter of a *bar* during the *aperitivo* hour or shelled in a delicate, lively colored gelato.

GELATO DI FIOR DI LATTE

Fior di latte (flower of milk), also the name used for fresh cow's milk mozzarella, might more aptly be called plain gelato. It is a delicate gelato made without any flavorings other than milk and sugar and is sometimes used as the base for other gelati. The color is a pale milky white rather than the eggy yellow of *gelato di crema. Fior di latte* is the first ice cream mothers give to their *bambini.*

ANTIPASTI

Nowhere is Florentine culinary tradition more evident than in *antipasti,*

small bites that tickle the appetite as the rest of the meal is prepared.

When you sit down at a trattoria, the most customary *antipasti* served are platters of chicken liver crostini and *affettati* (sliced cured meats). A popular springtime *antipasto* consists of fava (broad) beans eaten straight from their pods with soft, fresh pecorino. In autumn, jewel green *olio nuovo,* pungent olive oil fresh from the presses, is drizzled over slices of toasted Tuscan bread rubbed with garlic. *Sott'oli* (vegetables—especially artichokes—marinated in olive oil) and *sott'aceti* (pickled vegetables) evoke times past, when canning and pickling were the only ways for Florentines to preserve each season's bounty.

FRITTATA DI PORRI E ZUCCHINI
Leek and Zucchini Frittata

The expression fare una frittata *(make a frittata) is also used to convey "make a mess of things." The evolution of the saying is unclear, since frittatas are actually quite easy to make. Zucchini is one of the most popular fillings, but almost any leftover vegetables will do. Roasted red or yellow bell peppers (capsicums), sautéed mushrooms, or slices of cooked potato and fried onions could also be used. Italian eggs are usually very high quality, with bright orange yolks and dense whites. Some shopkeepers, especially in the country-side, have a basket of their own eggs somewhere under the till and will gladly sell you a few if you ask.*

8 very fresh large eggs

Salt and freshly ground pepper

3 leeks, white and pale green parts only

2 tablespoons butter

3 tablespoons extra-virgin olive oil

1 lb (500 g) zucchini (courgettes), halved lengthwise and thinly sliced

Handful of fresh basil leaves

Makes 4 servings

1 Preheat the broiler (grill) or preheat the oven to 400°F (200°C). In a bowl, lightly beat the eggs just until blended and season with salt and pepper.

2 Cut the leeks crosswise into small rings. Rinse in a colander, separating the rings to remove any trapped soil. Drain well.

3 In a large ovenproof frying pan over medium heat, melt the butter with the olive oil. Add the leeks and sauté until they begin to soften and release their juices, about 3 minutes. Add the zucchini and sauté until soft and lightly golden, 5–8 minutes, adding the basil leaves toward the end of cooking. Distribute the vegetables and basil leaves evenly over the bottom of the pan, then pour the beaten eggs over the top. Reduce the heat to low and cook slowly, occasionally running a spatula along the sides of the pan to keep the frittata from sticking, until the sides and bottom are set but the center is still loose, about 5 minutes.

4 Slip the pan under the broiler or transfer to the oven and cook until the top is firm and lightly golden, about 3 minutes. Cut into wedges and serve warm or at room temperature.

Serve with a young, fresh red wine such as Rosso di Montalcino or a full-bodied white wine such as a Tuscan Chardonnay.

BRUSCHETTE CON CANNELLINI E OLIO NUOVO

Bruschetta with White Beans and Olive Oil

White beans are a staple of the Florentine diet. During the summer, they are sold fresh in their weathered yellowed pods, and though the shucking takes awhile, the beans cook in a fraction of the time of their dried counterparts. By the time the olive harvest rolls around in midautumn, dried beans have filled the pantry. Nothing does greater justice to the sharp, fruity flavor of freshly pressed olive oil than a slice of toasted bread smothered with warm beans and generously doused with the pungent, new oil.

1 Pick over the beans, discarding any grit or misshapen beans. Rinse well, place in a large bowl, and add cold water to cover generously. Let soak overnight.

2 The next day, drain the beans, then rinse well and place them in a heavy soup pot. Add 8 cups (64 fl oz/2 l) water, 2 tablespoons of the olive oil, the garlic, the sage, and the peppercorns, cover, and bring to a simmer over medium heat. Reduce the heat so that the water simmers very gently and cook until the skins of the beans are tender and the interiors are soft, about 2 hours. Season to taste with salt three-fourths of the way through the cooking time. Remove the beans from the heat and let them cool slightly in their cooking water.

3 Preheat the oven to 375°F (190°C). Arrange the bread slices in a single layer on a baking sheet and bake until golden, 3–5 minutes.

4 Divide the toasts among individual plates. Ladle a generous amount of beans and a bit of the cooking water on each toast. Drizzle abundantly with some of the remaining olive oil, season to taste with salt and pepper, and serve.

Serve with a dry, chilled *vino rosato* (rosé).

2 cups (1 lb/500 g) dried cannellini beans (page 185)

8 tablespoons (4 fl oz/125 ml) extra-virgin olive oil

3 cloves garlic

1 fresh sage sprig

6–8 peppercorns

Salt and freshly ground pepper

4 slices coarse country bread, about ¾ inch (2 cm) thick

Makes 4 servings

Il Cotto

Along with its olive groves and vineyards, the countryside around Florence is famous for the soil itself—not the reddish brown topsoil that nourishes the harvest, but the ferrous gray layer below. When fired at temperatures upwards of 1800°F (1000°C), this earth yields what many consider to be the world's finest terra-cotta—or *cotto*, as it is called in Impruneta, the prosperous hilltown where the high quality of the soil and craftsmanship has made it a renowned center of terra-cotta manufacturing.

Impruneta's deep orange *cotto* is both hardworking and decorative. Its uses range from roofs and floors to intricately decorated vases. Perhaps nowhere is the form and function of Impruneta's *cotto* more beautiful than in the waist-high *orci*, elegantly curved urns used for storing olive oil. Many producers still keep their oil in *orci*, some of which are more than a century old. Smaller vessels such as the casserole-like *coccio* are considered the best choice for cooking many of Florence's most beloved dishes. Over coals, in the oven, or on the stove top, terra-cotta distributes heat uniformly and becomes seasoned with use.

INSALATA DI GALLINA
Poached Chicken Salad with Spicy Mayonnaise

Brodo di pollo, or chicken broth, has a number of uses in the Florentine kitchen. Foremost among them is as a base for risotto or for pastina in brodo (pasta in broth), a favorite comfort dish of most Italian children. At the bright and sunny Trattoria Zibibbo on the northern edge of Florence, chef and proprietor Benedetta Vitali (who first opened the celebrated Cibrèo restaurant in 1979 with her former husband, Fabio Picchi) puts the chicken used for making brodo to delicious use in this salad. Her homemade mayonnaise has the warm yellow color that comes from using the freshest farm eggs and golden Tuscan olive oil.

FOR THE CHICKEN

1 red onion

2 *each* celery stalks and carrots

1 tomato

1 chicken, about 2 lb (1 kg)

2 teaspoons sea salt

FOR THE MAYONNAISE

6 very fresh large egg yolks, at room temperature

Juice of 1 or 2 lemons

Pinch of salt, plus more to taste

1¼ cups (10 fl oz/310 ml) extra-virgin olive oil

2 tablespoons finely chopped fresh flat-leaf (Italian) parsley

1 teaspoon sweet paprika

Pinch of red pepper flakes

FOR THE SALAD

1 red bell pepper (capsicum)

¼ cup (2 fl oz/60 ml) extra-virgin olive oil

1 teaspoon *each* red wine vinegar and fresh lemon juice

6 cups (9 oz/280 g) mixed radicchio and chicory (curly endive) leaves

Makes 8 servings

1 To cook the chicken, coarsely chop the onion, celery, carrots, and tomato. Place the vegetables in a large soup pot and add 8 cups (64 fl oz/2 l) cold water. Bring to a boil over high heat, then add the chicken and sea salt. Add more water if necessary to cover the chicken completely and return to a boil. Reduce the heat to low and simmer, partially covered, for 1½ hours. Remove the chicken from the stock. Discard the vegetables and reserve the stock for another use. When the chicken is cool enough to handle, pull the meat off the bones and cut or shred into thin strips, discarding the skin.

2 To make the mayonnaise, in a large glass or stainless-steel bowl, whisk together the egg yolks, juice of 1 lemon, and pinch of salt. When the mixture is light and smooth, slowly whisk in half of the olive oil, a small amount at a time, adding more oil only when the previous amount has been fully absorbed. Taste and add more lemon juice and salt if needed. Add the remaining olive oil, in a steadier stream and whisking more vigorously, until the mayonnaise is smooth and silky; you may not need all of the oil. Stir in the parsley, paprika, and red pepper flakes. Cover and refrigerate until ready to use.

3 Remove the stem, ribs, and seeds from the bell pepper and cut the flesh into paper-thin strips. Set aside. To assemble the salad, in a large bowl, combine the olive oil, vinegar, and lemon juice. Whisk together with a fork. Add the radicchio and chicory and toss to coat very lightly. Arrange on a platter and scatter with the chicken. Spoon dollops of mayonnaise on top. Top with the reserved bell pepper strips and serve at once.

Serve with a lightly oaked white wine such as a Tuscan Chardonnay.

PROSCIUTTO, SALAME, MELONE E FICCHI

Prosciutto, Salami, Melon, and Figs

The ripe sweetness of melons and figs makes a perfect foil for cured Tuscan meats. Prosciutto and melon are the most traditional pairing. The prosciutto should be sliced to an almost transparent thinness so that its flavor does not overpower the delicate melon. Meloni—or poponi, as they are sometimes called in Tuscany—are strictly a summer fruit; out of season, they are expensive and insipid. Figs are undoubtedly the most sensual of all Tuscan fruits, making their short season—late summer, early autumn—all the more precious.

1 Arrange the figs in the center of a large serving platter. Roll each slice of salami into a loose cylinder and place around the figs.

2 Cut each melon half into 6 wedges, then cut the rind from each wedge. Arrange the melon on the platter. Drape with the slices of prosciutto. Serve with the bread alongside.

Serve with a crisp white wine such as Vermentino di Bolgheri.

12 fresh figs, halved lengthwise

½ lb (250 g) semi-aged Italian salami such as *salame toscano* (page 32), thinly sliced on a slight diagonal

1 large ripe cantaloupe, halved and seeded

6 oz (185 g) prosciutto (pages 32–33), sliced paper-thin

1 loaf coarse country bread, sliced

Makes 6 servings

Uno Spuntino

There are two extremes to taking *uno spuntino,* or a snack, in Florence, both equally sublime: the elegant and the earthy. The former is found just where you'd expect it, on the glamorous Via de' Tornabuoni. At Procacci, shoppers come from Gucci, Ferragamo, or one of the other temples to high fashion that line the famous street to sip a glass of Prosecco and nibble on delicate sandwiches filled with truffle paste or smoked salmon. The other extreme is well represented by I Fratellini. This tiny place near the Duomo would be easy to miss but for the crowd out front drinking local wine and eating crostini covered with wild mushrooms or simple sandwiches of pecorino, sun-dried tomatoes, and capers.

Falling somewhere in between is the Cantinetta di Verrazzano, a favorite spot to sit down for a snack and linger awhile. Verrazzano brings the Chianti wine region to the center of Florence. The Falorni butcher shop from the Tuscan town of Greve in Chianti supplies cured meats, and the Castello di Verrazzano winery contributes its award-winning wines.

TORTA SALATA CON BIETOLA

Savory Tart with Swiss Chard

The closer a food is to its source, the more Tuscans seem to like it. At any given season, but especially during spring and autumn, locals carrying baskets or bags comb the woods and fields searching for wild asparagus, mushrooms, and edible greens, including the humble dandelion, whose tangy flavor is perfect for this savory tart from La Corte Armonica. The restaurant, which opens onto a tranquil courtyard, specializes in organic vegetarian food, from traditional Tuscan to Indian and macrobiotic. This version of the tart calls for either Swiss chard or dandelion greens, since the latter may not be readily available.

FOR THE FILLING

Salt

2 lb (1 kg) Swiss chard or dandelion greens, stems and tough center stalks removed

6 tablespoons (3 fl oz/90 ml) extra-virgin olive oil

2 cloves garlic, crushed

¼ cup (2 oz/60 g) capers, rinsed and drained

¾ cup (3½ oz/105 g) brine-cured pitted black olives, drained and coarsely chopped

FOR THE PASTRY

1¾ cups (9 oz/280 g) all-purpose (plain) flour

½ teaspoon salt

½ teaspoon dried oregano

⅓ cup (3 fl oz/80 ml) extra-virgin olive oil, plus more for brushing

3 tablespoons dry white wine

⅓–½ cup (3–4 fl oz/ 80–125 ml) water

Makes 6–8 servings

1 To make the filling, bring a saucepan three-fourths full of water to a boil over medium heat. Lightly salt the water, add the greens, and boil until tender, about 8 minutes. Drain in a colander and set aside until cool enough to handle. Squeeze the greens to remove excess water, then chop finely and set aside.

2 In a heavy-bottomed frying pan over medium heat, warm the olive oil. Add the garlic and sauté until golden and fragrant, about 1 minute. Add the chopped greens and sauté for about 3 minutes. Add the capers and olives and cook, stirring frequently, until all the liquid has evaporated, about 7 minutes. Remove from the heat and let cool.

3 To make the pastry by hand, in a large bowl, whisk together the flour, salt, and oregano. Make a well in the center and pour in the olive oil. Rub the oil and dry ingredients between your fingers until the mixture takes on the consistency of wet sand. Add the wine and sprinkle in enough water, 1 tablespoon at a time, so the mixture forms a loose mass when stirred with a fork. To make the dough in a food processor, combine the flour, salt, and oregano. Pulse 3 or 4 times to blend. Add the olive oil and pulse until the mixture resembles wet sand. Add the wine and enough of the water so that the mixture begins to come together into a loose mass. Transfer to a lightly floured work surface and knead by hand until the dough becomes light and silky, 10–15 minutes. Shape the dough into a ball, cover with plastic wrap, and refrigerate for at least 30 minutes or up to overnight.

4 Preheat the oven to 375°F (190°C). Lightly oil and flour a 9- or 10-inch (23- or 25-cm) tart pan, preferably with a removable bottom.

5 Divide the dough into 2 balls, one slightly larger than the other. On a lightly floured work surface, roll the larger ball into a 12-inch (30-cm) round. Drape the dough over the rolling pin and ease it into the tart pan, gently pressing the dough into the edges of the pan. Trim the edge of the dough, leaving 1½–2 inches (4–5 cm) of overhang. Gently spoon in the filling and spread it evenly. Roll the second ball of dough into a 10-inch (25-cm) round, drape it over the rolling pin, and lay it over the filling. Moisten the edge of the bottom crust and crimp the edges of the top and bottom crusts to seal. Using a pastry brush, lightly brush the crust with olive oil. Pierce the surface of the tart in several places with a fork.

6 Bake until the top is lightly golden, 25–35 minutes. Transfer to a wire rack to cool. If using a pan with a removable bottom, remove the tart by placing the pan on a large aluminum can or canister and letting the sides fall away. Slide the tart onto a serving plate. Serve warm or at room temperature, cut into wedges.

Serve with a light, crisp *vino rosato* (rosé).

INSALATA GARGA

Arugula Salad with Pine Nuts, Avocado, and Hearts of Palm

When Trattoria Garga first opened over two decades ago, the prospect of finding anything more than a simple insalata verde *(cultivated or wild lettuces) or* insalata mista *(lettuce, tomato, carrot, and cucumber) on a restaurant menu was unlikely. Trattoria Garga changed all that with its signature* insalata, *which includes avocado and hearts of palm—both unusual ingredients in Florence. Today, owners Sharon Oddson and Giuliano Gargani's two sons run the trattoria, located on Via del Moro, and their well-loved signature* insalata *is still a favorite on the menu.*

1 In a salad bowl, toss together the arugula, tomatoes, pine nuts, hearts of palm, avocado, and Parmigiano-Reggiano.

2 To make the dressing, in a small bowl, whisk together the olive oil, lemon juice, and salt and pepper to taste. Pour over the salad and toss well. Serve at once.

Serve with a light, crisp *vino rosato* (rosé).

6 cups (6 oz/185 g) tender arugula (rocket) leaves

2 tomatoes, cut into small chunks

⅓ cup (2 oz/60 g) pine nuts

4 stalks canned hearts of palm, cut on a slight diagonal into ½-inch (12-mm) slices

1 ripe avocado, pitted, peeled, and cut into thin slices

2-oz (60-g) piece Parmigiano-Reggiano cheese, cut into thin shavings with a vegetable peeler

FOR THE DRESSING

6 tablespoons (3 fl oz/90 ml) extra-virgin olive oil

2 tablespoons fresh lemon juice

Salt and freshly ground pepper

Makes 4 servings

Arugula

Arugula, known both as *rucola* and *rughetta,* is a favorite Florentine salad green that is both cultivated and gathered wild in unplowed fields. The leaves have a sharp and piquant flavor. Spicier still is wild *rucola,* whose leaves are somewhat less tender than those of its cultivated cousin. Because of its strong flavor, arugula is generally mixed with other ingredients rather than eaten on its own. Italians scatter arugula leaves over slivers of raw baby artichokes and shaved Parmigiano-Reggiano cheese or toss them into salads of oranges, raw fennel, and pecorino cheese. The long, thin, deep green leaves are also used to enliven pizza, pasta, and grilled steaks.

Arugula leaves are sold in small bunches at the *fruttivendolo,* or greengrocer, and are a fixture in most Tuscan home vegetable gardens. It is one of the easiest and most satisfying salad greens to grow. Scatter the seeds over loamy soil and a dense patch of bright green leaves will appear within weeks. Harvest the leaves as needed, pinching them off the stem or cutting the stems at the ground—they will grow up again two more times before the leaves become too tough to eat.

CARCIOFI SOTT'OLIO
Marinated Artichoke Hearts

Delicatessens and gastronomie *throughout the city offer marinated artichokes behind their counters. They are delicious, to be sure, but they rarely measure up to homemade* carciofi sott'olio. *Preserving artichokes used to be the only way to eat them once their season had passed. Though olives tend to be prized more as a source for olive oil than for curing and eating, every farmers' market seems to have at least one* banco, *or stand, selling a variety of dry-cured and brined olives out of small wooden barrels. Serve both of these savory bites as part of a larger* antipasto *spread or as a snack between meals.*

1 bottle (24 fl oz/750 ml) dry white wine

1 cup (8 fl oz/250 ml) white wine vinegar

2 teaspoons coarse sea salt

10 peppercorns

4 *each* bay leaves and whole cloves

2 lb (1 kg) baby artichokes

1 lemon, halved

About 1½ cups (12 fl oz/375 ml) extra-virgin olive oil, plus more as needed

Makes 1 pint (16 fl oz/500 ml)

1 In a saucepan over high heat, bring the wine, vinegar, and salt to a boil with 4 of the peppercorns, 1 bay leaf, and 1 clove. Reduce the heat to low and simmer for 5 minutes.

2 Meanwhile, working with 1 artichoke at a time, pull off the outer leaves until you reach the tender yellow- and purple-tinged inner leaves. Using a knife, cut off the tough green tops of the leaves until only the tender, edible portion remains. Trim the stem to 1 inch (2.5 cm) and pare away the tough outer layer. Rub the stem and cut edges of each artichoke lightly with the cut side of a lemon half. When all the artichokes are ready, drop them into the wine mixture.

3 Return the wine mixture to a simmer and cook the artichokes for 10 minutes. Drain and pat dry. Fill a sterilized 1-pint (16–fl oz/500-ml) lidded jar with the artichokes, layering them with the remaining peppercorns, bay leaves, and cloves. Fill the jar with the 1½ cups olive oil, making sure no air pockets remain. Add additional olive oil to the jar as the contents settle. Close the jar tightly and store in a dark, cool place for 1 month before eating.

Serve with a refreshing white wine such as Vernaccia di San Gimignano.

OLIVE INSAPORITE
Spicy Black and Green Olives

2 cups (10 oz/315 g) mixed unpitted olives in brine

2 cloves garlic, thinly sliced

1 tablespoon finely chopped fresh flat-leaf (Italian) parsley

1 teaspoon coriander seeds

½ teaspoon red pepper flakes

Grated zest of ½ lemon

3 or 4 black peppercorns, crushed

¼ cup (2 fl oz/60 ml) extra-virgin olive oil

Makes 2 cups (10 oz/315 g)

1 Drain the olives and place them in a ceramic or glass bowl. Add the garlic, parsley, coriander seeds, red pepper flakes, lemon zest, peppercorns, and olive oil. Toss the mixture well.

2 Cover the bowl and let the mixture marinate at room temperature for at least 2 hours or for up to 24 hours before serving.

Serve with a light white wine such as Verdicchio.

SCHIACCIATA AL RAMERINO E SALVIA

Flatbread with Rosemary and Sage

At the Antica Dolce Forneria in San Casciano, the Caioli family makes schiacciata *three times a day so that it will always be warm from the oven whether wrapped to take to school or eaten as an afternoon* merenda *(snack). Proper Tuscan bakers like the Caiolis use* pasta acida, *a sourdough starter developed over a period of weeks that gives the dough a pleasantly tangy smell and yields a wonderfully chewy texture. Though the starter in this recipe is made overnight, it still yields a bread with old-world results. The exact flour and water measurements will vary slightly according to humidity and the age of the flour.*

1 To make the starter, in a bowl, dissolve the yeast in the lukewarm water. Let the mixture stand for 10 minutes. Using a wooden spoon, stir in the flour and water and mix until a rough ball forms. Transfer to a lightly floured work surface and knead until the starter becomes smooth and elastic, about 10 minutes. Place in a large, lightly oiled bowl, turn the starter once to coat with the oil, then cover the bowl with a damp kitchen towel. Let the starter rise at room temperature for 8 hours or up to overnight.

2 To make the dough, in a large bowl, mix together the starter, flour, and water. When the dough forms a cohesive mass, transfer to a lightly floured work surface and knead until smooth and elastic, about 10 minutes. Place in a large, lightly oiled bowl, turn the dough once to coat with the oil, then cover the bowl with a damp kitchen towel. Let the dough rise in a warm spot in the kitchen until it more than doubles in volume, about 4 hours.

3 Punch the dough down, fold in its outer edges, and turn the dough over. Cover the bowl again with a damp kitchen towel and let rise for 2 hours longer.

4 Preheat the oven to 450°F (230°C). Place a baking sheet on the bottom of the oven to create extra heat from below. Dust a second baking sheet with flour.

5 Transfer the dough to a lightly floured work surface and knead for about 2 minutes. Flatten the dough into an 8-by-12-inch (20-by-30-cm) rectangle about 1 inch (2.5 cm) thick. Gently lay it on the prepared baking sheet. Using your fingertips, dimple the surface of the dough, spacing the dimples about 1½ inches (4 cm) apart. Using a pastry brush, coat the top of the dough with about 2 tablespoons of the olive oil. Sprinkle evenly with the salt, sage, and rosemary leaves.

6 Bake until golden on top, about 25 minutes. Transfer to a wire rack. When the *schiacciata* has cooled slightly, drizzle with the remaining 2 tablespoons olive oil. Cut into pieces and serve warm.

FOR THE STARTER

Pinch of active dry yeast

⅓ cup (3 fl oz/80 ml) lukewarm (95°F/35°C) water

2 cups (10 oz/315 g) bread flour

1 cup (8 fl oz/250 ml) water, at room temperature

FOR THE DOUGH

3 cups (15 oz/470 g) bread flour

¾ cup (6 fl oz/180 ml) water, at room temperature

4 tablespoons (2 fl oz/60 ml) extra-virgin olive oil

1 teaspoon salt

Handful of fresh sage leaves

Leaves of 1 fresh rosemary sprig

Makes 1 large flatbread

CROSTINI DI FEGATINI DI POLLO

Chicken Liver Crostini

Throughout Italy, crostini generally refers to thin slices of bread covered with a spread or paste of some kind. The quintessential crostini in and around Florence—and the ones implied whenever they are listed on a menu without further explanation—are spread with a version of chicken liver pâté. Some cooks use milza, or spleen, in their recipes, while others use a dash of Cognac or even vin santo. This outstanding recipe comes from Sostanza, one of the city's most beloved restaurants. Alongside a platter of cured meats, crostini are the most typical way to begin a traditional Florentine meal.

1 tablespoon butter

3 tablespoons extra-virgin olive oil

1 yellow onion, finely chopped

½ lb (250 g) chicken livers, trimmed and passed through a meat grinder or minced

1 salt-cured anchovy fillet (page 185), rinsed and minced

1½ teaspoons capers, rinsed, drained, and minced

Juice of ½ lemon

Salt and freshly ground pepper

1 baguette, cut on a slight diagonal into ½-inch (12-mm) slices

Makes 4 servings

1 In a saucepan over medium heat, melt the butter with the olive oil. Add the onion and cook, stirring frequently and adding a few teaspoons of water if necessary to keep the onion from browning, until soft and translucent, about 10 minutes. Add the chicken livers, anchovy, capers, and lemon juice and stir well to combine. Add 2 cups (16 fl oz/500 ml) water and bring to a boil. Reduce the heat to low and simmer gently until the mixture has the consistency of a thick, moist sauce, about 1½ hours. Season to taste with salt and pepper.

2 The chicken liver pâté can be served warm or cold (to reheat, place the pâté in a saucepan over medium heat and add a bit of water if the consistency has thickened too much). Divide the baguette slices among individual plates. Top with the pâté and serve the crostini at once.

Serve with a spicy, young red wine such as Chianti Classico.

INSALATA DI BACCELLI E PECORINO

Fava Bean and Pecorino Cheese Salad

Fava beans, or baccelli, *as they are called in Florence, are one of the first vegetables of the Tuscan spring garden. Early in the season, the beans are so crisp and tender they are eaten raw, straight out of their bright green pods, often paired with* marzolino, *a fresh sheep's milk cheese traditionally made in* marzo *(March), hence its name. Informal lunches often begin with a heaping basket of unshelled beans, a round of soft, tart* marzolino, *and a few thick slices of country bread. For this* baccelli *and cheese salad, use a slightly older pecorino, which will hold its shape better when cut.*

1 If using young, tender fava beans, use your thumb to split the fava bean pods along their seams and shell the beans directly into a salad bowl.

2 If using more mature fava beans, shell them and set aside. Bring a pot three-fourths full of water to a boil. Add the reserved beans and blanch for about 2 minutes. Drain and let cool. Pinch each bean to slip it from its skin. Discard the skins and transfer the beans to a salad bowl.

3 Cut the cheese into ½-inch (12-mm) cubes and add the cubes to the bowl along with the fava beans. Add the olive oil, a light sprinkling of salt,

and freshly ground pepper to taste to the cheese and beans. Toss all the ingredients together and serve the salad at once.

Serve with a light, honeyed red wine such as Morellino di Scansano.

Note: Florentines would only make this dish using very fresh, young fava beans. But if they are unavailable, you can use more mature beans if you blanch and peel them first.

3 lb (1.5 kg) fresh, tender fava (broad) beans in their pods (see Note)

6 oz (185 g) medium-aged pecorino cheese

¼ cup (2 fl oz/60 ml) extra-virgin olive oil

Salt and freshly ground pepper

Makes 4 servings

PRIMI

The *primo*, or first course, whether a hearty soup, a humble bread salad,

or a crisp, elegant risotto cake, is often the best part of the meal.

The rest of the world may equate Italian *primi* with heaping plates of spaghetti, but in Florence and much of Tuscany, nothing makes for a better *primo,* or first course, than a bowl of soup. *Pappa al pomodoro* (tomato and bread soup) and *ribollita* ("twice-cooked" bread and vegetable soup) are two of the city's most beloved recipes made from day-old saltless Tuscan bread and local vegetables. Florentines also enjoy Italian standards like pasta, risotto, and polenta. Every home cook has his or her own recipe for *sugo* (meat sauce) and can assemble a pasta sauce with little more than a splash of *olio di oliva* and a handful of fresh vegetables.

PIZZA CON MOZZARELLA, CIPOLLA E RUCOLA

Pizza with Mozzarella, Onion, and Arugula

On any given night, Pizzeria Lo Spela, on the Grevigiana road leading from Florence to the wine town of Greve in Chianti, is packed to the rafters. Owner Paolo Pannacci was Lo Spela's pizzaiolo (pizza maker) for fourteen years before buying the place from its previous owner, who still comes by to help wait on tables on especially busy nights. Asked for the secrets to his success, Pannacci smiles. "No secrets. I like a pizza so thin that it's crisp as a cracker around the edges, with the cheese golden and bubbly in the center. I use an oak fire, which burns hot and slow, and mozzarella fior di latte, pure cow's milk mozzarella."

FOR THE PIZZA DOUGH

3 cups (12 oz/375 g) cake (soft-wheat) flour, plus more for dusting

1 package (1½ teaspoons) active dry yeast dissolved in ⅓ cup (3 fl oz/80 ml) warm water (105°–115°F/40°–46°C)

⅔ cup (5 fl oz/160 ml) warm water (105°–115°F/40°–46°C)

1 teaspoon salt

1 teaspoon extra-virgin olive oil

1¾ cups (10 oz/315 g) canned puréed plum (Roma) tomatoes

1 lb (500 g) fresh mozzarella cheese, shredded or sliced

1 large yellow onion, sliced paper-thin

4 cups (4 oz/120 g) tender arugula (rocket) leaves

Makes 4 pizzas or 4 servings

1 To make the pizza dough, place the flour in a mound on a clean flat work surface and make a well in the center. Pour the dissolved yeast mixture and the ⅔ cup warm water into the well. Use one hand to swirl the liquid in a circular motion, gradually incorporating flour from the sides of the well. When a rough mass forms, add the salt. Continue to incorporate the flour gradually, then add the olive oil and incorporate only enough of the remaining flour to render the dough just soft but not sticky. Shape the dough into a ball. Clean the work surface and dust generously with flour. Knead the dough until smooth and elastic, 7–10 minutes. If the dough sticks to your hands, add a bit more flour. If it feels too dry, sprinkle with water.

2 Cover the dough with a damp kitchen towel and let rest for 5 minutes. Divide into 4 balls, cover again with a damp kitchen towel, and let rise at room temperature until doubled in bulk, about 3½ hours.

3 Place a pizza stone or unglazed tiles in the oven and preheat to the hottest setting (500° or 550°F/260° or 290°C).

4 Lightly flour the work surface, leaving a mound of flour to one side to take from as needed. Place 1 of the dough balls on the work surface and leave the others under the damp towel. Press down on the dough ball with your fingers to form a flat disk. Turn the disk over, sprinkle with additional flour, and, using a rolling pin, roll out the dough into a 10-inch (25-cm) round, turning the dough over periodically and dusting it regularly with flour. Use your hands to stretch it gently into a 12–14-inch (30–35-cm) round.

5 Lightly sprinkle a baker's peel or an inverted baking sheet with flour. Gently lay the dough round on top. Spread evenly with one-fourth of the puréed tomatoes. Scatter one-fourth of the mozzarella and one-fourth of the onion slices on top. Slide the pizza onto the pizza stone or tiles and bake until the cheese is melted and the crust is browned and crisp, 5–8 minutes. Roll out and prepare each of the remaining pizzas as the previous one bakes.

6 As each pizza is removed from the oven, scatter with 1 cup (1 oz/30 g) arugula leaves. Serve, then slip the next pizza into the oven.

Serve with a classic Italian beer such as Moretti.

FARRO CON CALAMARETTI, RUCOLA E POMODORI CILIEGINI

Farro with Squid, Arugula, and Cherry Tomatoes

This recipe comes from Il Guscio, a restaurant in Florence's San Frediano quarter not far from the spectacular Masaccio frescoes in the Capella Brancacci. When making this summery salad, "use squid only as big as the size of your hand," counsels chef-proprietor Elena Baglioni. The bodies of larger squid and cuttlefish are best stuffed with fillings, while those of smaller squid are ideal for cutting into rings and have delicate tentacles more suitable for salads. Take care not to overcook the squid or it will become tough and chewy.

1 In a saucepan over high heat, bring 3 cups (24 fl oz/ 750 ml) water to a boil. Add the *farro,* reduce the heat to low, cover partially, and simmer until the *farro* is tender but still firm, about 20 minutes. Drain well and set aside.

2 To clean the squid, working with one at a time, pull the head and tentacles from the body pouch. Discard the clinging innards. Cut off the tentacles just below the eyes and discard the eye portion. Squeeze the cut end of the tentacles to expel the hard beak and discard. Pull the long, transparent quill from inside the body pouch and discard. Remove and discard the gray membrane covering the body pouch. Rinse the pouch and tentacles under cold running water. Repeat to clean the remaining squid.

3 In a saucepan fitted with a steamer basket, bring about 1 inch (2.5 cm) of water to a boil over high heat. Reduce the heat to low, place the squid in the basket, cover, and steam until tender, 3–5 minutes. When the squid are cool enough to handle but still warm, cut the pouches crosswise into ½-inch (12-mm) rings and the tentacles into 1-inch (2.5-cm) sections.

4 Combine the *farro,* squid, arugula, and tomatoes in a serving bowl. Add the olive oil and lemon juice and toss to combine. Season to taste with salt and pepper and serve at once.

Serve with a light, crisp white wine such as Vernaccia di San Gimignano.

1 cup (5 oz/155 g) pearled *farro*

1 lb (500 g) squid

2 cups (2 oz/60 g) tender arugula (rocket) leaves

½ lb (250 g) cherry tomatoes, quartered

⅓ cup (3 fl oz/80 ml) extra-virgin olive oil

Juice of 1 lemon

Salt and freshly ground pepper

Makes 4 servings

Farro

Farro—or *far,* as it was called in ancient times when the Romans cultivated it to feed to their legions—is one of the world's oldest grains, used throughout the Mediterranean for millennia in soups, porridges, and breads. Over time, it was replaced throughout most of Italy by wheat, which was found to be better suited for making the pasta and breads Italians so adore. *Farro* is still grown in small pockets of Italy, most famously in the wild hills of the Garfagnana above the stunning fortified town of Lucca, where it thrives at altitudes under 3,000 feet (900 m) in poor soil otherwise unsuitable for planting. Much of the *farro* grown here is organic and high in protein, with a deliciously nutty, wheatlike flavor.

Farro grains are oval shaped, with a long groove running down their length. The skin is a muddy brown color, concealing a pale, floury interior that becomes plump and starchy as it absorbs liquid during cooking. Pearled *farro,* or *farro perlato,* has had the outer hull polished off and cooks more quickly. Tuscans use *farro* like barley in soups, or cooked and cooled as the base for *panzanella*-inspired tossed salads.

PENNE CON PESCE SPADA E MELANZANE
Penne with Swordfish and Eggplant

"The origins of this dish are Sicilian," explains Arturo Dori, chef and proprietor of Il Cavolo Nero, a sophisticated and intimate restaurant in Florence's atmospheric San Frediano quarter. Dori's pasta dish is a welcome change from the city's more tried-and-true primi, *such as* ribollita *or* pappa al pomodoro. *Though fish is not always associated with Florence, you can certainly find plenty of fresh fish—mostly Mediterranean—at the Mercato Centrale (page 23) and at fishmongers around town. The firm flesh of swordfish holds up well to cooking, making it perfectly suited for this first course.*

1 large globe eggplant (aubergine)

¾ lb (375 g) swordfish fillets

6 tablespoons (3 fl oz/90 ml) extra-virgin olive oil

1 clove garlic, minced

1 teaspoon chopped fresh flat-leaf (Italian) parsley

Pinch of red pepper flakes

Salt

¾ lb (375 g) penne

½ cup (4 fl oz/125 ml) dry white wine

Pinch of dried oregano

Makes 4 servings

1 Slice the eggplant lengthwise as thinly as possible. Stack 2–3 slices on top of each other and cut into 1-inch (2.5-cm) squares. Repeat to cut the remaining eggplant slices in the same way. Cut the swordfish into 1-inch (2.5-cm) cubes. Bring a large pot three-fourths full of water to a boil.

2 In a large frying pan over medium-low heat, warm 3 tablespoons of the olive oil. Add the garlic, parsley, and red pepper flakes and sauté briefly to release the flavors, about 1 minute; do not let the garlic brown. Raise the heat to medium, add the eggplant, and sauté until the eggplant is tender but still firm, about 5 minutes. Transfer to a bowl and set aside.

3 Salt the boiling water, add the penne, and cook until al dente, about 10 minutes.

4 Meanwhile, add the remaining 3 tablespoons olive oil to the frying pan over medium-high heat. When the oil is hot but not smoking, add the swordfish cubes and sauté briefly until the fish is opaque on all sides, about 4 minutes. Add the wine and cook until the alcohol evaporates, about 2 minutes. Add the reserved eggplant mixture, reduce the heat to medium, and cook until well blended, about 2 minutes. Add the oregano and stir to combine. Remove from the heat.

5 When the pasta is ready, drain, reserving about 1 cup (8 fl oz/250 ml) of the cooking water. Add the pasta to the sauce and heat over high heat for 1–2 minutes, stirring to combine. Add a bit of the reserved cooking water from the pasta if the mixture seems too dry. Serve at once.

Serve with a delicate white wine such as Vernaccia di San Gimignano.

TAGLIATELLE AI FUNGHI PORCINI

Tagliatelle with Porcino Mushrooms

When the soil is damp and spongy and the weather just right, neither too hot nor too cold, locals take to the woodlands carrying baskets and long wooden sticks. They are searching for mushrooms, using their staffs to overturn leaves in hopes that something edible lies underneath. Of all wild mushrooms, none except perhaps the rare orange-capped ovolo is as prized as the fungo porcino (porcino mushroom). Locals cook porcini with nepitella, a small-leaved wild mint, but they are delicious, as here, with fresh thyme.

1 Cut away the tips of the mushroom stems; if using shiitake mushrooms, discard the entire stem. Thinly slice the mushrooms lengthwise.

2 In a large, heavy-bottomed frying pan over medium heat, warm the olive oil. Add the garlic and sauté until golden and fragrant, about 2 minutes. Remove and discard the garlic. Add the mushrooms and sauté, stirring with a wooden spoon, until they begin to soften, 3–4 minutes. (They might stick to the pan for a moment before beginning to release their juices, but it is not necessary to add more oil.) Raise the heat to high, add the wine and thyme, and cook, stirring constantly, until the alcohol from the wine has evaporated, about 3 minutes. Reduce the heat to low, season to taste with salt and pepper, and continue to cook, stirring often, until the mushrooms are cooked through and all the liquid has evaporated, about 15 minutes longer.

3 Meanwhile, bring a large pot three-fourths full of water to a boil. Salt the boiling water, add the tagliatelle, and cook until al dente, about 8 minutes. Drain, reserving about 1 cup (8 fl oz/250 ml) of the cooking water.

4 When the mushrooms are ready, remove from the heat and stir in the butter. Add the pasta and toss, adding a bit of the reserved cooking water if the pasta seems too dry. Serve at once with grated Parmigiano-Reggiano.

Serve with a spicy, rich red wine such as Vino Nobile di Montepulciano.

2 lb (1 kg) fresh porcino mushrooms or other wild or cultivated mushrooms such as shiitake or cremini, brushed clean

⅓ cup (3 fl oz/80 ml) extra-virgin olive oil

4 cloves garlic, crushed

½ cup (4 fl oz/125 ml) dry white wine

3 or 4 fresh thyme or *nepitella* (calamint) sprigs (page 186)

Salt and freshly ground pepper

1 lb (500 g) spinach tagliatelle, or a mixture of spinach and egg tagliatelle

2 tablespoons butter

Freshly grated Parmigiano-Reggiano cheese for serving

Makes 4–6 servings

Culinary Adventures

Cooking schools abound in and around Florence, but most of them aim to endow their students with the same standard know-how behind the region's most traditional recipes. When Peggy Markel founded La Cucina al Focolare (Cooking by the Fireside) in 1991, her goal was to offer a culinary adventure. She set up shop in a fifteenth-century farmhouse overlooking the Arno valley, where she teamed up with chef Piero Ferrini to take students through a deep course in preparing bread soups, cooking in a wood-fired oven, making biscotti, and more.

Hands-on cooking is only part of the experience. Markel is as likely to take her students on mushroom hunts in the local woods as she is to spend time with them ambling around farmers' markets and paying visits to her friends: Pierre, the French herb grower–philosopher; Sandro, the master baker who moonlights as an opera singer; and Tillo, whose Corzano e Paterno cheese must be tasted to be believed. These and other masters of their culinary crafts share a passion for what they do and never fail to inspire Markel's adventurers.

RAVIOLI DI RICOTTA CON POMODORI

Ricotta Ravioli with Fresh Tomatoes

No one is certain how many centuries ago water buffalo were brought to southern Italy from India, but everyone agrees that their sweet milk is especially suited to the making of mozzarella cheese and to its by-product, ricotta cheese. As its name implies, ricotta is made by "recooking" the whey left after making mozzarella or other cheeses. At Alle Murate, one of Florence's most elegant restaurants, delicate ricotta di bufala is used to fill homemade ravioli. Cow's milk ricotta makes a fine substitution. The addition of ground cinnamon softens the tartness of the tomatoes.

FOR THE FILLING

1¼ cups (10 oz/315 g) whole-milk ricotta cheese

1 large egg

½ cup (2 oz/60 g) freshly grated Parmigiano-Reggiano cheese

1½ teaspoons ground cinnamon

Salt and freshly ground pepper

FOR THE PASTA DOUGH

3 cups (15 oz/470 g) all-purpose (plain) flour, plus more for dusting

Pinch of salt

4 large eggs

2 teaspoons extra-virgin olive oil

FOR THE SAUCE

¼ cup (2 fl oz/60 ml) extra-virgin olive oil

4 cloves garlic, crushed

1½ lb (750 g) plum (Roma) tomatoes, peeled and seeded (page 187), then coarsely chopped

Salt and freshly ground pepper

Handful of fresh basil leaves

Freshly grated Parmigiano-Reggiano cheese for serving

Makes 6 servings

1 To make the filling, in a bowl, combine the ricotta, egg, Parmesan, and cinnamon, and season with salt and pepper. Blend with a wooden spoon until smooth.

2 To make the pasta dough, place the flour in a mound on a clean flat work surface and make a well in the center. Sprinkle with the salt. Break the eggs into the center of the well, add the olive oil, and beat lightly with a fork. Use one hand to swirl the egg mixture in a circular motion, incorporating flour from the sides of the well. When a rough mass forms, shape it into a ball and set it on top of the remaining loose flour. Using both hands, work the remaining flour into the dough, incorporating only enough of the flour so that the dough just barely stops sticking to your fingers. Set aside. Clean the work surface and dust lightly with flour. Knead the dough until it is smooth and elastic, 6–8 minutes, adding more flour if the dough is sticky. If rolling the dough by hand, wrap it tightly in plastic wrap and let rest at room temperature for at least 20 minutes or for up to 3 hours. If using a pasta machine, the dough may be rolled out immediately.

3 To roll out the dough with a pasta machine, follow the manufacturer's directions until the dough has reached the narrowest setting. To roll by hand, unwrap the dough and cut it in half. Briefly knead one-half, then lightly dust the work surface and a rolling pin with flour. Place the dough in the center of the surface and press into a thick, flat round. Roll out to a uniform round, then turn over, lightly flour the rolling pin, and roll out until the dough is a thin, even round. The dough is thin enough if your hand is visible through it when it is held up to the light. Set the dough aside on a lightly floured kitchen towel. Repeat with the remaining dough. Use a straight-edged pizza cutter to cut the rolled-out dough into strips 3 inches (7.5 cm) wide.

4 To assemble the ravioli, place heaping teaspoons of the filling along the upper center of the length of 1 strip, spacing them 1½ inches (4 cm) apart and stopping within 1 inch (2.5 cm) of the ends. Brush the edges around the filling with water, then fold the strip over to enclose the filling. Seal each mound of filling by using your fingertips to press out any air. Use a fluted pastry wheel to cut 1½-inch (4-cm) filled squares. Transfer to a flour-dusted baking sheet. Repeat with the remaining dough and filling. Bring a large pot three-fourths full of water to a boil.

5 Meanwhile, make the sauce: In a frying pan over medium-low heat, warm the olive oil. Add the garlic and sauté until golden, about 1 minute. Add the tomatoes. Raise the heat to medium and bring to a simmer, stirring occasionally. Reduce the heat to low, season to taste with salt and pepper, add the basil leaves, and simmer until the tomatoes thicken into a light sauce, about 7 minutes. Keep warm.

6 Salt the boiling water, add the ravioli, and cook until al dente, 3–4 minutes; test a ravioli after 3 minutes. Drain the ravioli and divide among shallow individual bowls. Spoon the sauce over the ravioli and serve at once, with grated Parmigiano-Reggiano.

Serve with a spicy, elegant red wine such as Chianti Classico Riserva.

PANZANELLA
Bread Salad

Because of the belief that nothing, not even the humblest slice of old bread, should go to waste, the Florentine table displays dishes that use pane sciocco, *the saltless country bread that is the city's staff of life, in every season. In summertime,* panzanella *is a favorite first course, and recipes for this salad of bread, red onion, cucumber, and juicy fresh tomatoes abound. La Vecchia Bettola, a quintessential trattoria just outside the city's ancient walls on the edge of the lively San Frediano quarter, makes a delicious version.*

1 In a large bowl, combine 4 cups (32 fl oz/1 l) water and the vinegar. Add the bread slices and let soak for 10–15 minutes. Drain well, then squeeze out all the excess liquid from the bread. Crumble into bite-sized pieces and place in a large salad bowl.

2 Add the lettuce, onion, cucumber, tomatoes, basil, ¼ cup olive oil, and salt and pepper to taste. Toss well (Florentines always use their hands for this task). Taste and add a little more olive oil, if desired. Serve at room temperature or chilled.

Serve with a brisk, young red wine such as Chianti.

1 cup (8 fl oz/250 ml) red wine vinegar

6 slices 2- to 3-day-old coarse country bread, preferably unsalted

1 head romaine (cos) lettuce, cored and coarsely chopped

1 sweet onion, such as Maui or Tropea, thinly sliced

1 cucumber, peeled, halved lengthwise, seeded, and thickly sliced

3 tomatoes, coarsely chopped

2 generous handfuls of fresh basil leaves

¼ cup (2 fl oz/60 ml) extra-virgin olive oil, or as needed

Salt and freshly ground pepper

Makes 4 servings

Tomatoes

Pomodori are divided into two categories in Italy: cooking tomatoes and salad tomatoes (a few species fit both categories). The cooking stalwarts *pomodori a grappolo* hang heavily in bunches from a central stem. These are the workhorses, available year-round, used primarily for sauces but also in salads by those who can't wait until salad tomatoes are in season. *Ciliegini* are sweet cherry tomatoes that hang in clusters like grapes on the vine. *Bambini* love *ciliegini*, perhaps because they are perfectly sized for hungry, young mouths. Florence has its own cooking tomato, the appropriately named *fiorentino,* a deep red fruit with pleated skin and dense, sweet flesh.

Pomodori insalatari—salad, or "eating," tomatoes—can be a surprise for first-time visitors to Italy. They often look unripe, their skins in various stages of turning from green to red, and they are not uniform in size or shape, like tomatoes in markets in the United States and elsewhere. Deciding on which tomatoes to purchase at the height of the season may involve inspecting as many as ten varieties—and always includes much discussion between buyer and grocer.

LINGUINE A' MASANIELLO
Linguine with Shellfish

In southern Italy, especially in Naples, frutti di mare (shellfish) are ubiquitous, enjoyed in such dishes as shellfish sautéed with garlic and wine and linguine heaped with mussels, prawns, and clams. Angelo Taddio's Il Pizzaiuolo, on the edge of the Sant'Ambrogio market, has brought the south's traditions to Florence. His pizza is Neapolitan style (thick and chewy from well-leavened dough). His seafood pastas, such as this one—named after a famed Neapolitan revolutionary—with its abundance of shellfish flavored with tomatoes, wine, and a hint of hot red pepper, bring the Mediterranean to the Florentine table.

⅓ cup (3 fl oz/80 ml) extra-virgin olive oil

2 cloves garlic, minced

Salt

1 lb (500 g) linguine

1 lb (500 g) small clams such as Manila or littleneck, soaked for 2 hours in several changes of lightly salted water

½ lb (250 g) mussels, scrubbed and debearded

4 large or 8 medium shrimp (prawns), about ½ lb (250 g) total weight, preferably in their shells

Pinch of red pepper flakes

1 cup (8 fl oz/250 ml) dry white wine

2 tablespoons chopped fresh flat-leaf (Italian) parsley

½ cup (3 oz/90 g) cherry tomatoes, halved

Makes 4 servings

1 In a large frying pan over medium heat, warm the olive oil. Add the garlic and sauté until lightly golden and fragrant, about 2 minutes.

2 Bring a large pot three-fourths full of water to a boil. Salt the water, add the linguine, and cook until al dente, 7–9 minutes.

3 Meanwhile, add the clams and mussels to the frying pan, discarding any that do not close to the touch. Add the shrimp and the red pepper flakes. Stir the shellfish until warmed but not yet open, about 2 minutes, then raise the heat to medium-high and add the wine, parsley, and tomatoes. Use a wooden spoon to crush the tomato halves in the pan. Cook until the clam and mussel shells open and the shrimp are opaque beneath their pink shells, about 4 minutes. Remove from the heat and discard any clams or mussels that failed to open. Transfer the shellfish and sauce to a large, shallow serving bowl.

4 When the pasta is ready, drain, reserving about 1 cup (8 fl oz/250 ml) of the cooking water. Toss the pasta with the shellfish and sauce, adding a bit of the reserved cooking water if the pasta seems too dry. Serve at once.

Serve with a crisp, dry white wine such as Val di Cornia Bianco.

Note: Florentines would purchase shrimp with their heads and legs to make this dish. If you prefer, use shrimp with their heads and legs removed but shells intact. (Shrimp cooked with their shells are more flavorful.)

GNUDI DI RICOTTA E SPINACI AL TARTUFO
Ricotta and Spinach Dumplings with Truffles

Gnudi (pronounced "nudie") are essentially spinach and ricotta ravioli without their clothes on, that is, without pasta. During spring, Francesco Altomare of Ristorante Oliviero serves them with melted butter and tartufi bianchetti marzolini, *white spring truffles from San Miniato, near Siena. "Our Tuscan truffles are much more affordable than the white truffles of the Piedmont," he says, "but still have that pungent, earthy flavor truffle lovers adore." If you can't find truffles, drizzle the* gnudi *with truffle oil and top with Parmesan shavings.*

1 Place the ricotta in a colander lined with cheese-cloth (muslin) and let stand for 10–15 minutes to drain off any liquid.

2 Put the spinach with just the rinsing water clinging to the leaves in a large soup pot over medium heat. Cook, covered, until soft and wilted, about 5 minutes. Drain and let cool. Form the spinach into a ball, squeezing out as much liquid as possible. Chop the spinach very finely by hand or by pulsing in a food processor. Again squeeze out any liquid. Bring a large pot three-fourths full of water to a boil.

3 Meanwhile, in a large bowl, combine the whole egg, egg yolks, drained ricotta, and spinach. Add the grated Parmigiano-Reggiano, 2 tablespoons flour, and nutmeg, and season with salt and pepper. Use your hands to combine the ingredients until a thick, homogenous paste forms. Form and roll into 1½-inch (4-cm) balls and dust them lightly with flour. The balls will be soft, but if they are too soft to hold their shape, cover and refrigerate for about 30 minutes.

4 Salt the boiling water. Using a slotted spoon, slide the *gnudi* into the water. Cook until they float to the top, about 3 minutes. Use the spoon to transfer the *gnudi* to a warmed serving bowl. Toss gently with the melted butter. If using fresh truffles, use a truffle shaver or vegetable peeler to thinly slice the truffles over the top. If using truffle oil, drizzle it over the *gnudi* and top with the Parmigiano-Reggiano shavings. Serve at once.

Serve with a rich red wine such as a Super Tuscan blended from Sangiovese and Cabernet Sauvignon.

FOR THE GNUDI

1¼ cups (10 oz/315 g) whole-milk ricotta cheese

1 bunch spinach, about 1 lb (500 g), stems removed

1 large egg plus 2 large egg yolks, lightly beaten

1 cup (4 oz/125 g) freshly grated Parmigiano-Reggiano cheese

2 tablespoons all-purpose (plain) flour, plus more for dusting

Pinch of freshly ground nutmeg

Salt and freshly ground pepper

4 tablespoons (2 oz/60 g) butter, melted

1½ oz (45 g) fresh white truffles, brushed clean, or 2 tablespoons white truffle oil

2-oz (60-g) piece Parmigiano-Reggiano cheese, cut into thin shavings with a vegetable peeler (if using truffle oil)

Makes 6 servings

Truffles

Truffles—or *tartufi* in Italian—are the gastronomic darlings of kings, poets, epicures, and almost anyone with the good fortune to have inhaled their seductive scent. Botanically, truffles are subterranean fungi that grow in symbiosis with the roots of certain wood-land plants, most famously oak trees, where they can be found only with much work and a good truffle-seeking dog or pig. The two most prized varieties are the white truffle, from the Piedmont in Italy, and the black truffle, found in Umbria, parts of Spain, and the Périgord region of France. Though unattractive—they look a bit like small, muddy stones—truffles are one of the most expensive foods on earth.

Fortunately, truffles are eaten as much with the nose as with the palate, since their scent seems to impart as much flavor as their substance. As a result, a small amount goes a long way, and just a few thin truffle shavings over pasta, risotto, meats, or fried eggs are enough to impart the fungi's sublime flavor and scent. If fresh truffles are unavailable, try using truffle-scented olive oil or whole preserved black truffles.

PAPPA AL POMODORO
Tomato and Bread Soup

Pappa al pomodoro is a fixture on menus in virtually every traditional Florentine restaurant. It combines a handful of ingredients locals love most: ripe summer tomatoes, bread (usually day old), olive oil, and basil. At Beccofino, near the banks of the Arno River, Scottish restaurateur David Gardner and his chef-partner Francesco Berardinelli give the soup an innovative cosmopolitan flair, topping it with grilled langoustines, croutons, fried basil leaves, and a drizzling of basil oil. The recipe here omits the shellfish but still features the bright green basil oil and crisp-fried basil leaves used as a garnish.

FOR THE BASIL OIL

1 cup (1 oz/30 g) packed fresh basil leaves

¾ cup (6 fl oz/180 ml) extra-virgin olive oil

FOR THE SOUP

6 tablespoons (3 fl oz/90 ml) extra-virgin olive oil, plus more for drizzling

3 celery stalks, minced

3 white onions, minced

2 carrots, peeled and minced

2 cloves garlic, minced

2 tablespoons tomato paste

2 lb (1 kg) plum (Roma) tomatoes, peeled and seeded (page 187), then coarsely chopped

1 teaspoon sugar

Salt and freshly ground pepper

1 lb (500 g) coarse country bread, preferably unsalted, crusts removed

Makes 4–6 servings

1 To make the basil oil, bring a small saucepan of water to a boil and have ready a bowl of ice water. Set aside 8 to 12 of the basil leaves and blanch the remaining leaves in the boiling water for about 10 seconds. Drain, then plunge into the ice water. Drain again, and squeeze the leaves to remove as much water as possible. Transfer to a blender, add the ¾ cup olive oil, and pulse until the mixture becomes a uniform deep green color. Strain the basil oil through a fine-mesh sieve lined with cheesecloth (muslin) and set aside.

2 Preheat the oven to 350°F (180°C). To make the soup, in a large saucepan over medium heat, warm 4 tablespoons (2 fl oz/60 ml) of the olive oil. Add the celery, onions, carrots, and garlic and sauté until the vegetables are softened but not browned, about 10 minutes. Stir in the tomato paste and continue to cook for 5 minutes longer.

3 Add the tomatoes and sugar and season to taste with salt and pepper. Simmer over medium heat, stirring occasionally, until the sugar has dissolved and the tomatoes are softened, about 10 minutes.

4 Meanwhile, cut the bread into 1½-inch (4-cm) cubes. Arrange in a single layer on a baking sheet, season with salt and pepper, and drizzle with olive oil. Bake until lightly toasted, about 10 minutes.

5 Add the toasted bread cubes and 6 cups (48 fl oz/ 1.5 l) water to the saucepan. Stir to combine with the vegetables, bring to a simmer over medium-high heat, and cook, uncovered and stirring often, until the bread has softened, about 15 minutes. Whisk the soup vigorously to break up the bread cubes. Taste and adjust the seasoning. Set aside and keep warm.

6 In a small frying pan over medium heat, warm the remaining 2 tablespoons olive oil. Add the reserved basil leaves and fry, turning once, until crisp and slightly transparent, about 30 seconds. Using tongs, carefully transfer to paper towels to drain and cool.

7 Ladle the soup into warmed individual bowls. Lay a couple of fried basil leaves on top of each portion, drizzle with a little basil oil (reserve the remainder for another use), and serve.

Serve with a chilled white wine such as a Tuscan Chardonnay or with a simple red wine such as Chianti Classico.

RISOTTO AL SALTO ALLA PARMIGIANA IN SALSA DI ZAFFERANO

Parmesan Risotto Cakes with Saffron Sauce

Trattoria Donnini began its life as an old-fashioned restaurant not far from the city on a quiet road winding into the country. Like many such trattorias, at its entrance was a deli counter brimming with prosciutto, salami, bread, and cheeses. A few tables in a bright room behind the storefront offered simple lunches from a small menu. Today's Donnini, while having retained its deli counter, is a graceful eatery with a wide, shady veranda for warm-weather meals and such elegant dishes as these delicate Parmesan rice cakes served with a saffron sauce.

1 To make the risotto, in a saucepan over medium heat, bring the stock to a gentle simmer. Adjust the heat to maintain a bare simmer.

2 In a separate large, heavy-bottomed saucepan over low heat, melt 1½ tablespoons of the butter. Add the onion and sauté until softened and lightly golden, about 5 minutes. Raise the heat to medium, add the rice, and stir with a wooden spoon until the grains are coated with the butter and lightly toasted, about 3 minutes. Add the wine and stir constantly until the rice completely absorbs the liquid.

3 Reduce the heat to medium-low, add a ladleful of the hot stock, and stir constantly until the rice absorbs the liquid. Continue adding small ladlefuls of stock, stirring constantly and waiting until the stock is absorbed before adding the next ladleful. When the rice is tender but still quite firm, after about 15 minutes, stir in the Parmigiano-Reggiano and season to taste with salt and pepper. Remove from the heat.

4 Transfer the rice to a bowl. Stir in the remaining 1½ tablespoons butter, and let the risotto cool, stirring occasionally, until stiff and easy to handle. Divide the rice into 4 equal portions. Line a baking sheet with parchment (baking) paper. Place each portion of risotto onto the sheet and use a spatula to form into disks about 4 inches (10 cm) in diameter and 1 inch (2.5 cm) thick. Cover the pan with plastic wrap and refrigerate until completely cool and firm, about 1 hour.

5 Meanwhile, make the sauce: In a small, heavy-bottomed saucepan over low heat, warm the cream and milk until bubbles form around the edges, about 3 minutes; do not let boil. In another saucepan over low heat, melt the 1 tablespoon butter. Sprinkle in the flour and stir constantly until the mixture thickens and has a faint toasty fragrance but is not browned, 2–3 minutes. Pour the hot cream mixture over the butter and flour mixture, whisking constantly and scraping around the edges to keep the mixture from sticking or forming lumps. Stir in the saffron and season to taste with salt. Continue whisking until the mixture forms a pale yellow sauce thick enough to flow in a slowly dissolving ribbon when the spoon is lifted, 3–4 minutes longer.

6 In a large, nonstick frying pan over medium heat, melt the 2 tablespoons butter with the olive oil. Carefully arrange the risotto cakes in the pan and cook, turning once, until they are heated through and golden and crisp on both sides, about 4 minutes on each side.

7 To serve, pour a small pool of the saffron sauce onto warmed individual plates. Place a risotto cake on each plate, cover with a drizzling of additional sauce, garnish with 3 Parmigiano-Reggiano shavings and some of the parsley, and serve at once.

Serve with an elegant white wine such as an oaked Chardonnay from Tuscany or the Aosta Valley.

FOR THE RISOTTO

4 cups (32 fl oz/1 l) beef or chicken stock

3 tablespoons butter

½ white onion, minced

1 cup (7 oz/220 g) Carnaroli rice (page 185)

2 tablespoons dry white wine

¼ cup (1 oz/30 g) freshly grated Parmigiano-Reggiano cheese

Salt and freshly ground pepper

FOR THE SAUCE

⅓ cup (3 fl oz/80 ml) *each* light cream and whole milk

1 tablespoon butter

2 tablespoons all-purpose (plain) flour

Large pinch of saffron threads

Salt

2 tablespoons butter

1 tablespoon olive oil

12 thin shavings Parmigiano-Reggiano cheese

2 tablespoons coarsely chopped fresh flat-leaf (Italian) parsley

Makes 4 servings

CREMA DI CECI CON FARRO E FUNGHI PORCINI
Puréed Chickpea Soup with Farro and Porcino Mushrooms

"Recipes are precious, you know?" said Guendalina Prosperi, as she handed me the instructions for making the soup her family serves at their Osteria San Niccolò. In true Florentine fashion, her words revealed neither reticence nor arrogance. She was simply stating a fact: Florence is filled with treasures, and this is one of them. Every ingredient in this warming soup represents Tuscany, from the dried beans and fresh herbs to the farro *and porcino mushrooms. Once you have tried this hearty recipe, you will understand the appeal of* cucina povera *(regional peasant cooking), the source of many traditional Tuscan soups.*

1½ cups (9½ oz/295 g) dried chickpeas (garbanzo beans)

⅓ cup (3 fl oz/80 ml) extra-virgin olive oil

1 yellow onion, finely chopped

2 cloves garlic, minced

1 small fresh rosemary sprig

1 tablespoon tomato paste

Salt and freshly ground pepper

4 cups (32 fl oz/1 l) vegetable stock or water

⅓ cup (2 oz/60 g) pearled *farro* (page 97)

FOR THE MUSHROOMS

½ lb (250 g) fresh porcino or cremino mushrooms, brushed clean

1½ tablespoons extra-virgin olive oil

1 clove garlic, crushed

2 tablespoons dry white wine

1 fresh thyme or *nepitella* (calamint) sprig (page 186)

Salt and freshly ground pepper

1½ teaspoons butter

Makes 4–6 servings

1 Place the chickpeas in a large bowl and add cold water to cover generously. Let soak overnight.

2 Drain the chickpeas, then rinse well and transfer to a large saucepan. Add 8 cups (64 fl oz/2 l) cold water and bring to a boil over high heat. Reduce the heat to low and simmer, uncovered, until the chickpeas are tender, about 2 hours. Set aside.

3 In a soup pot over medium-low heat, warm the olive oil. Add the onion, garlic, and rosemary and sauté until the onion is softened and translucent but not browned, about 6 minutes. In a small bowl, dissolve the tomato paste in 1 cup (8 fl oz/250 ml) warm water and add to the pot. Stir in the chickpeas and their cooking liquid and season to taste with salt and pepper. Bring to a simmer over medium heat and cook for 3 minutes. Add the stock, return to a simmer, and cook, uncovered, until the flavors have melded, about 30 minutes longer. Remove and discard the rosemary sprig. Blend the soup with an immersion or stand blender until smooth and creamy. (If desired, pass through a fine-mesh sieve for the smoothest consistency and return to the pot.) Return the soup to a simmer over medium heat, add the *farro,* and cook until the *farro* is tender but still firm, about 25 minutes.

4 Meanwhile, prepare the mushrooms: cut away the tips of the mushroom stems. Thinly slice the mushrooms lengthwise. In a large, heavy-bottomed frying pan over medium heat, warm the olive oil. Add the garlic and sauté until golden and fragrant, about 2 minutes. Remove and discard the garlic. Add the mushrooms and sauté, stirring with a wooden spoon, until they begin to soften, 3–4 minutes. (They might stick to the pan for a moment before beginning to release their juices, but it is not necessary to add more oil.) Raise the heat to high, add the wine and thyme, and cook, stirring constantly, until the alcohol from the wine has evaporated, about 3 minutes. Reduce the heat to low, season to taste with salt and pepper, and continue to cook, stirring often, until the mushrooms are cooked through and their juices have evaporated, about 15 minutes longer. Remove from the heat and stir in the butter. Discard the thyme sprig.

5 Add the mushrooms to the soup and stir to combine. Ladle the soup into warmed individual bowls and serve at once.

Serve with a savory red wine such as Chianti Classico Riserva or Carmignano Riserva.

POLENTA CON RAGÙ DI CARNE

Polenta with Beef Ragù

While polenta's indisputable domain is Italy's Veneto region in the north, Florentines have their uses for the ground cornmeal as well. Sometimes it is cooked and cooled, then cut into thin slices, fried, and used like the bread in bruschetta. When still warm and soft, it's best heaped with a hearty sauce like this beef ragù with porcino mushrooms served at Fuori Porta, a wine bar whose name (literally, "outside the door") refers to its location just outside the San Niccolò door into the old center of the city.

1 To make the ragù, in a saucepan over medium heat, warm the olive oil. Add the onion, carrot, celery, and garlic and sauté until softened, about 15 minutes. Add the sage leaves and beef, using a spoon to break up the beef. Distribute the meat evenly in the pan. Season with pepper, then raise the heat to high and stir well. When the meat is evenly browned, add the wine and cook until the alcohol has evaporated, about 3 minutes. Stir in 1½ cups (12 fl oz/375 ml) cold water and the bay leaf. Bring to a boil, scraping the sides of the pan occasionally. Reduce the heat to low, partially cover, and simmer, stirring occasionally, until the meat has released all its juices, about 45 minutes. Season with salt and pepper. Stir in the tomatoes and mushrooms, return to a simmer, and cook over low heat until the sauce is a medium consistency, about 45 minutes longer. Adjust the seasoning, set aside, and keep warm.

2 To make the polenta, in a heavy-bottomed saucepan over high heat, bring 7 cups (56 fl oz/1.75 l) water to a boil. Add the salt and pour in the polenta in a fine, steady stream, whisking constantly. Reduce the heat to medium. When the polenta begins to thicken, after about 5 minutes, reduce the heat to low. Cook, stirring constantly, until the polenta comes away easily from the sides of the pan, 30–40 minutes longer.

3 Divide the polenta among warmed individual bowls, ladle with a generous portion of the ragù, and serve at once. Pass the Parmigiano-Reggiano at the table.

Serve with a robust but elegant red wine such as a Cabernet Sauvignon from Bolgheri.

FOR THE RAGÙ

¼ cup (2 fl oz/60 ml) extra-virgin olive oil

1 yellow onion, finely chopped

1 large carrot, peeled and finely chopped

1 celery stalk, finely chopped

1 clove garlic, minced

3 fresh sage leaves

1½ lb (750 g) lean ground (minced) beef

Salt and freshly ground pepper

½ cup (4 fl oz/125 ml) dry white wine

1 bay leaf

1 can (14½ oz/455 g) crushed plum (Roma) tomatoes

3 oz (90 g) fresh porcino or cremino mushrooms, brushed clean and sliced

FOR THE POLENTA

2 teaspoons salt

1⅔ cups (8½ oz/265 g) coarse-ground polenta, preferably Italian

Freshly grated Parmigiano-Reggiano cheese for serving

Makes 6 servings

Wine Bars

The stratospheric rise in the quality and reputation of Tuscan wine has spawned a new breed of *vinai* (wine merchants). Their cellars might rival those of the city's best restaurants, but these wine bars are temples to *il vino* rather than *la cucina*. This doesn't mean there's nothing to eat, only that the food is there to exalt the wine rather than the reverse.

Fuori Porta was one of the first, and best, of the new wine bars. It looks rather like a casual restaurant, with outdoor tables overlooking the Porta San Niccolò and the high city walls leading up to the Forte di Belvedere. Here Andrea Conti offers an outstanding selection of wines by the glass and a *carta di vini* to make wine lovers swoon (or at the very least run to Fuori Porta's wine shop next door).

Le Volpi e L'Uva, tucked into the Piazza de' Rossi, is the place to go to taste wines you didn't even know existed, many from small wineries. Not only will owners Emilio Monecchi and Riccardo Comparini offer you a sampling of exquisite local and imported cheeses and cured meats, but they will happily dispense as much enological insight as you wish to hear.

RIBOLLITA
Twice-Cooked Vegetable Soup

Ribollita is Tuscany's most famous soup. Like so many local recipes, it has its origins in frugality. Leftover zuppa, most often made with white beans and durable winter vegetables (including cavolo nero, the deep green local cabbage), is baked in the oven—thus "reboiled" or twice cooked—with day-old bread. The resulting hearty soup is then seasoned with olive oil and black pepper. Trattoria Cammillo, which began as a wine shop in 1945, is justifiably famous for its version. If cavolo nero is not available, kale makes a fine substitution. Be sure to drizzle extra-virgin olive oil over each serving.

½ cup (4 fl oz/125 ml) extra-virgin olive oil, plus more for seasoning

2 carrots, peeled and coarsely chopped

2 celery stalks, chopped

2 yellow onions, coarsely chopped

2 potatoes, peeled and cut into chunks

2 zucchini (courgettes), coarsely chopped

1 cup (6 oz/185 g) canned plum (Roma) tomatoes, chopped

1 bunch *cavolo nero* (page 185) or kale, tough center stalks removed, cut into thick strips

½ head savoy cabbage, coarsely chopped

1 bunch spinach, stemmed and coarsely chopped

3 cups (21 oz/655 g) cooked cannellini beans (page 185), prepared according to the recipe on page 73, or canned cannellini beans

Leaves from 3 fresh thyme sprigs

Salt and freshly ground pepper

5 slices day-old coarse country bread, preferably unsalted, toasted

Makes 6–8 servings

1 In a soup pot over medium heat, warm the ½ cup olive oil. Add the carrots, celery, onions, potatoes, and zucchini and sauté until the vegetables are softened, 10–15 minutes. Stir in the tomatoes and 4 cups (32 fl oz/1 l) water, then add the *cavolo nero*, savoy cabbage, and spinach. Raise the heat to high, bring to a simmer, reduce the heat to low, and let cook until the greens are tender, about 45 minutes.

2 Stir in the beans and cook over medium heat for 10 minutes longer. Add the thyme leaves and season to taste with salt and pepper. Remove from the heat and let cool, then cover and refrigerate overnight.

3 The following day, preheat the oven to 350°F (180°C). Line a 2-qt (2-l) baking dish with the toasted bread slices and ladle the soup over the top.

Bake, stirring occasionally with a wooden spoon so that the bread slices break apart and blend with the soup, 20–25 minutes. Continue baking without stirring until a lightly browned crust forms on top of the soup, 5–10 minutes longer.

4 Serve at the table directly from the dish. Season generously with olive oil and freshly ground pepper.

Serve with a dry red wine such as Chianti Classico.

SECONDI

In keeping with true Tuscan culinary spirit, the *secondi*, or main courses,

served in Florence are simple but succulent, often roasted or grilled meats.

Rumors abound as to the origins of *bistecca alla fiorentina,* the city's most famous *secondo.* One attributes the name to an exclamation: "Beef steak!" allegedly was the response of a group of sixteenth-century Englishmen who wandered into Piazza San Lorenzo and marveled at the sight of huge slabs of beef roasting over embers in the night. *Carne alla brace,* meat cooked over coals, is another favorite in Florence, as are slow-cooked meats like *coniglio* (rabbit), osso buco, and beef braised in red wine. The city's distance from the sea historically made fresh fish a luxury, so *baccalà* (salt cod) became the staple for meatless Fridays.

BOCCONCINI DI VITELLA AL RABARBARO E MIELE

Veal with Rhubarb-Honey Sauce

Enoteca Pinchiorri's head chefs, Italo Bassi and Riccardo Monco, preside over a kitchen staff of eighteen. The restaurant's cucina is every cook's dream: spacious, much less ferociously hot than most, and filled with the highest-quality equipment, all of it strategically placed so as to allow the kitchen's elaborate culinary dance to unfold seamlessly. The restaurant serves this veal with a mousse of potatoes, cream, and egg that is fashioned into small balls and wrapped in bright green spinach leaves.

1 Place the rosemary sprig in a bowl with the olive oil and let marinate overnight at room temperature.

2 The following day, cut the veal into 1¼-inch (3-cm) cubes. Add to the bowl with the olive oil and rosemary and marinate, covered, in the refrigerator for at least 3 hours or for up to 8 hours.

3 To make the rhubarb-honey sauce, use a small knife to peel away any strings on the rhubarb stalks. Cut the stalks crosswise into 1-inch (2.5-cm) pieces. Place them in a small saucepan and add 1 cup (8 fl oz/ 250 ml) water and the butter. Bring to a simmer over medium-low heat, stirring often, and cook until almost all the liquid has evaporated, about 20 minutes. Remove from the heat. When the mixture has cooled, blend to a paste with an immersion or stand blender. Stir in the honey and season to taste with salt and pepper. Refrigerate the sauce until it becomes dense and creamy, about 2 hours. Bring to room temperature before cooking the veal.

4 Heat a frying pan over medium heat. Drain the veal cubes, discarding the marinade, and add to the pan. Season the veal with the paprika and salt and pepper. Cook, stirring often, until the meat is lightly browned on all sides, about 5 minutes.

5 Divide the rhubarb-honey sauce among warmed individual plates. Arrange the veal on top, sprinkle with the minced rosemary, and serve at once.

Serve with a crisp, dry, citrusy white wine such as Vermentino di Bolgheri.

1 fresh rosemary sprig, leaves lightly crushed with a pestle

3 tablespoons extra-virgin olive oil

1½ lb (750 g) veal tenderloin

FOR THE RHUBARB-HONEY SAUCE

2 stalks rhubarb, about ½ lb (250 g) total weight, trimmed

6 tablespoons (3 oz/90 g) butter

2 tablespoons honey

Salt and freshly ground pepper

Pinch of sweet paprika

Salt and freshly ground pepper

1½ teaspoons minced fresh rosemary

Makes 4 servings

Enoteca Pinchiorri

The Enoteca Pinchiorri is quite unlike any other restaurant in the whole of Florence—or, for that matter, almost in the whole of Italy. It belongs to an elite coterie of world-class, Michelin-star restaurants. The wine cellars are stocked with thousands of bottles, and exquisitely wrought food arrives at the table with a great (but never overbearing) flourish on fine porcelain dishes covered with silver domes. The chandeliers here are Murano glass, the stemware Riedel, and the artwork and statuary truly authentic, all bringing a Medicean splendor to an extraordinary modern dining experience.

Giorgio Pinchiorri and his Niçoise wife, Annie Féolde, opened the restaurant in 1972 on the ground floor of a grand palazzo on the Via Ghibellina. Summertime brings dishes like rock lobster grilled with raisins and marjoram; risotto scented with lemon and turmeric; and duck breast with apple and thyme to their menu. Annie developed two tasting menus, and Giorgio created a variety of exceptional wine pairings. Expect to pay for the privilege of such sumptuous grandeur, but consider it an investment in an experience you will never forget.

POLLO ARROSTO AL LIMONE
Lemon Roasted Chicken

It is one thing to say that simplicity is the essence of the Tuscan kitchen. It is quite another to taste the extraordinary deliciousness that can come from just one chicken, two lemons, and a pinch of salt and pepper. "Of course, the chicken must be the freshest free-range and the lemons organic," says Patty Castano of Trattoria I Ricchi in the hills of Monte Morello, just north of Florence. The place began as a neighborhood food shop in 1929 and has been a favorite Florentine gastronomic escape since 1964. Serve this dish with roasted-garlic mashed potatoes for a favorite weeknight meal.

1 chicken, about 3½ lb (1.75 kg), preferably free-range, neck and giblets removed

2 tablespoons extra-virgin olive oil

Salt and freshly ground pepper

2 small lemons, preferably organic

Makes 4 servings

1 Preheat the oven to 375°F (190°C). Rinse the chicken inside and out. Pat dry with paper towels. Rub the outside of the chicken with the olive oil, then sprinkle the skin and cavity with salt and pepper. Stuff the cavity with the 2 whole lemons. Tuck the wings behind the back. Draw the drumsticks together and tie tightly with kitchen string.

2 Lightly oil a shallow roasting pan large enough to hold the chicken comfortably. Place the chicken, breast side up, in the pan and roast, basting occasionally with the juices, until it is deep golden brown and the juices run clear when a thigh is pierced with a sharp knife, about 1¼ hours. An instant-read thermometer inserted into the thickest part of a thigh away from the bone should register 170°F (77°C).

3 Transfer the chicken to a carving board and set the roasting pan aside. Remove the lemons from the cavity and set aside. Loosely tent the chicken with aluminum foil and let rest for 10 minutes.

4 When the lemons are cool enough to handle, cut them in half and squeeze the juice into the roasting pan. Discard the lemons. Add 3 tablespoons water to the juices in the pan. Place over high heat and cook until reduced by one-third, about 2 minutes.

5 Remove the string, carve the chicken, and arrange on a warmed serving platter. Pour the pan juices over the top and serve at once.

Serve with a young red wine such as Rosso di Montepulciano or a crisp white wine such as a Tuscan Chardonnay.

TAGLIATA DI MANZO

Grilled Florentine Steak

Tagliata refers to something cut, in this case the gargantuan bistecca alla fiorentina. A tagliata is the perfect gastronomic solution for the meat lover who cannot imagine tackling an entire bistecca on his or her own. A scattering of shaved Parmesan and arugula is a favorite way of dressing up a tagliata. Expect a Florentine chef to want to cook your tagliata as tradition dictates: well browned on the outside and red on the inside, so that each cut releases a stream of juices onto the plate.

1 Remove the meat from the refrigerator 2 hours before grilling.

2 Prepare a medium-hot fire in a grill and let burn until the coals are covered with white ash. Leave the coals heaped in the center of the grill; do not spread them out. If using a gas grill, preheat on medium-high.

3 Using tongs (to avoid piercing the meat), set the steaks on the grill, if possible at a slight angle, about 5 inches (13 cm) above hot, but not flaming, coals (or over the heating element of the gas grill). This will keep the dripping fat from igniting the coals. Grill until the first side is well browned, 5–7 minutes. Turn the steaks over, sprinkle with salt, and cook for 5–7 minutes longer. Turn the steaks again and sprinkle with salt. The meat should be well browned on both sides and pink and juicy inside.

4 Transfer the steaks to a cutting board and cut across the grain into ½-inch (12-mm) slices, removing the bone. Arrange the slices on a serving platter and top with any juices accumulated on the cutting board. Season generously with freshly ground pepper, scatter the arugula and Parmigiano-Reggiano on top, drizzle with olive oil, and serve.

Serve with a velvety Cabernet Sauvignon from Bolgheri or a dark, rich Chianti Classico Riserva.

2 T-bone or porterhouse steaks, each about 1¾ lb (875 g) and 1½ inches (4 cm) thick

Salt and freshly ground pepper

2 cups (2 oz/60 g) tender, young arugula (rocket) leaves

2-oz (60-g) piece Parmigiano-Reggiano cheese, cut into thin shavings with a vegetable peeler

Extra-virgin olive oil for drizzling

Makes 4 servings

Bistecca alla Fiorentina

The formula for an authentic *bistecca* is not complicated so much as it is exact. Ideally the meat should come from Chianina cattle, an ancient breed of giant white oxen. Specialty butchers and some restaurants have access to Chianina meat, but even in Florence it is not readily available. The meat should be well aged and cut to the height of *due dita* (two fingers held sideways), or about 1½ inches (4 cm). The cut itself is a porterhouse or T-bone, which contains both the fillet and the top loin.

More than a century ago, Pellegrino Artusi, Italy's greatest food writer, offered a few guidelines for preparing this most famous of Florentine *secondi* in his encyclopedic *La scienza in cucina e l'arte di mangiar bene*. First, the meat should be cooked over hot, but not flaming coals. (Florence's trattoria Sostanza tilts the grill slightly so that any fat dripping off the meat will not ignite the coals.) It should be seasoned simply with salt and pepper, and only after cooking, as preseasoning may dry out the meat. Lastly, it should never be dressed with olive oil until after grilling, or the steak will take on a tallowlike taste.

FILETTI DI ROMBO AL FORNO CON CARCIOFI

Baked Turbot with Artichokes

Although Florence is only an hour from the sparking waters of the Mediterranean, fresh seafood is rarely featured on most restaurant menus. Inzimino (squid or cuttlefish braised with chard or spinach) and baccalà (salt cod) are the standard exceptions to this rule. The elegant Ristorante Don Chisciotte is one of the handful of Florentine restaurants that base their menus almost entirely on seafood. Chef Walter Viligiardi is especially adept at wedding the sea's bounty with the finest local seasonal vegetables. This recipe pairs turbot fillets with artichokes and fresh herbs to create a light and satisfying main course.

Juice of ½ lemon

2 large artichokes

4 tablespoons (2 fl oz/60 ml) extra-virgin olive oil

1 clove garlic, minced

Salt and freshly ground pepper

1½ lb (750 g) turbot, sole, or flounder fillets

4 fresh marjoram sprigs

1 cup (8 fl oz/250 ml) dry white wine

Makes 4 servings

1 Preheat the oven to 350°F (180°C). Add the lemon juice to a bowl of cold water. Working with 1 artichoke at a time, pull off the outer leaves until you reach the pale, tender inner leaves. Using a knife, cut off the tough green tops of the leaves until only the tender, edible portion remains. Trim the stem to 1 inch (2.5 cm) and pare away the tough outer layer. Cut each artichoke in half lengthwise and use a spoon to remove the hairy choke. Cut each artichoke half into 4 wedges and place in the bowl of lemon water until ready to use.

2 In a small frying pan over low heat, warm 2 tablespoons of the olive oil. Add the garlic and sauté until golden, about 2 minutes. Drain the artichokes and scatter the wedges evenly in the pan. Add ⅓ cup (3 fl oz/80 ml) water and season with salt and pepper.

Bring to a boil, reduce the heat to low, cover, and simmer gently for 20 minutes, adding a bit more water to the pan if it is drying out.

3 Oil a baking dish large enough to hold the fillets in a single layer. Place the fillets in the dish and cover evenly with the artichokes, marjoram, and any oil in the bottom of the frying pan. Pour the wine on top, drizzle with the remaining 2 tablespoons olive oil, and bake until the fillets are opaque throughout, about 10 minutes. Divide the fillets and artichokes among warmed individual plates. Spoon any juices left in the dish over the top and serve at once.

Serve with a buttery white wine such as a Tuscan Chardonnay or a crisp, flinty Soave.

SCAMERITA COL CAVOLO NERO
Pork with Tuscan Black Cabbage

Tucked into the tangle of narrow streets and alleyways in the center of Florence is Coco Lezzone, one of the city's best-loved restaurants and originator of this recipe. "This dish is so hearty, we serve it only during winter," explains owner Luca Paoli. Historically, Tuscan frugality has deemed virtually any cut of meat or offal, including tripe (see right), worthy of being eaten. Scamerita is a relatively inexpensive cut of pork, perfect for slow cooking. Pork blade steaks from the neck end rather than the center loin can also be used.

1 Bring a large pot three-fourths full of salted water to a boil. Cut away the center stalks of the *cavolo nero* and pull out any tough fibers running through the leaves. Add the leaves to the boiling water, reduce the heat to low, cover, and simmer until very soft, about 1 hour. Drain and let stand until cool enough to handle. Squeeze to remove as much water as possible from the leaves. Chop coarsely and set aside.

2 In a frying pan over medium-low heat, warm 2 tablespoons of the olive oil. Add 2 of the garlic cloves and sauté until lightly golden, about 2 minutes. Raise the heat to medium, add the pork, season with salt and pepper, and cook until brown on both sides, about 6 minutes total. Remove from the heat and set aside.

3 In a large frying pan over medium heat, warm the remaining 3 tablespoons olive oil. Add the remaining 4 garlic cloves and sauté until lightly golden, about 2 minutes. Remove and discard the garlic. Add the tomatoes, using a wooden spoon to break them into pieces. Season to taste with salt and pepper and simmer, stirring occasionally, until the mixture forms a thick sauce, about 20 minutes.

4 Lay the pork steaks in an even layer over the tomatoes, cover with the *cavolo nero,* and cook over medium heat until the flavors have melded and the pork is fork-tender, about 30 minutes. Divide the pork and *cavolo nero* among individual plates and serve at once.

Serve with a noble, elegant red wine such as a Super Tuscan made from 100 percent Sangiovese.

Salt and freshly ground pepper

3 lb (1.5 kg) *cavolo nero* (page 185) or kale

5 tablespoons (3 fl oz/80 ml) extra-virgin olive oil

6 cloves garlic, crushed

4 pork blade steaks or center loin chops, about ½ lb (250 g) each

1 can (14½ oz/455 g) plum (Roma) tomatoes

Makes 4 servings

La Trippa

La trippa is the lining of any of the first three chambers of a ruminant's stomach, usually a young ox, though sometimes a pig or sheep. The milky white honey-combed tripe from the second stomach, pleasantly chewy and subtly flavored, is the local favorite in Florence. *Lampredotto,* the fourth stomach, is darker in color and lighter in texture. Florence's tripe vendors are easily identifiable. Just look for a cart bearing a pair of steaming cauldrons and surrounded by a small crowd of people contentedly nibbling away on *lampredotto* sandwiches, tripe salad, *trippa* with butter and Parmesan, or *trippa* cooked in a tomato sauce with artichokes, potatoes, or white beans.

When a customer sidles up to the narrow counter and asks for "un panino…piccante con salsa verde," the *trippaio* will assemble a sandwich with a generous layer of *lampredotto;* a spoonful of fresh parsley, olive oil, and garlic sauce; a dash of red pepper flakes; and a pinch of salt, and then hand it over the counter along with a paper cup of red wine. A visit to the *trippaio* is a quintessentially Florentine experience, and one that can be had for less than the price of a fast-food meal.

STRACOTTO AL PÈPPOLI

Braised Beef with Pèppoli Wine

Florence can overwhelm—its art and culture sent the French writer Stendhal into such a swoon that the romantic malady "Stendhal's Syndrome" was coined for him. The Antinori winemaking family's Cantinetta Antinori offers a perfect respite for the overawed. Nestled in a courtyard off the Via de' Tornabuoni (home to such famed designer boutiques as Gucci and Ferragamo), the restaurant is a haven of sophistication and tranquility, serving classic Tuscan food and, naturally, the full selection of Antinori wines. The Cantinetta uses its Pèppoli wine for this dish, but any quality Chianti Classico will do nicely.

2½ lb (1.25 kg) rump or chuck steak, in 1 piece

1½ oz (45 g) pancetta (page 186), cut into small dice

2 carrots, peeled and finely chopped

½ celery stalk, finely chopped

Salt and freshly ground pepper

½ cup (4 fl oz/125 ml) extra-virgin olive oil

2 yellow onions, finely chopped

3 cloves garlic, finely chopped

1 tablespoon finely chopped fresh sage

1 tablespoon finely chopped fresh rosemary

1 bottle (24 fl oz/750 ml) Pèppoli or other Chianti Classico wine

⅓ cup (3 oz/90 g) tomato paste

1 can (14½ oz/455 g) plum (Roma) tomatoes, chopped

Makes 6 servings

1 Using a small, sharp knife, make about a dozen small incisions on one side of the meat. Fill the incisions with the pancetta and some of the chopped carrot and celery. Season the meat with salt and pepper, then roll it into a cylinder and tie it tightly with kitchen string at 2-inch (5-cm) intervals.

2 In a heavy Dutch oven large enough to hold the meat comfortably, warm ¼ cup (2 fl oz/60 ml) of the olive oil over medium heat. Add the onions, garlic, sage, rosemary, and remaining chopped carrot and celery. Sauté until the garlic is fragrant and golden, about 10 minutes. Add the remaining ¼ cup olive oil. When the oil is hot but not smoking, add the meat and cook until brown on all sides, turning it regularly so it does not stick to the pan, about 6 minutes. Pour the wine over the meat in ½-cup (4–fl oz/125-ml) increments, letting the alcohol in each increment evaporate before adding more wine and continuing to turn the meat frequently. Spread the tomato paste on the meat and cover with the chopped tomatoes.

3 Cover the pan and cook over medium heat, turning the meat occasionally and adding a bit of water as necessary to keep the sauce juicy, until the meat is very tender, 2–2½ hours.

4 Transfer the meat to a carving board and loosely tent with aluminum foil. Tilt the pan and spoon off the fat from the sauce. Strain the sauce through a medium-mesh sieve into a small saucepan, and warm over medium heat. Remove the kitchen string and cut the meat into ¼-inch (6-mm) slices. Divide among individual plates, top with the sauce, and serve at once.

Serve with a complex, spicy Chianti Classico Riserva.

CONIGLIO CON OLIVE E PINOLI

Rabbit with Olives and Pine Nuts

Growing grapes and olives, tending the vegetable garden, and raising enough chickens and rabbits to keep the family well stocked in eggs and meat typified the lives of Tuscan massaie (homemakers) of old. Rabbit is still almost as commonly eaten as chicken in Tuscany, and is considered more tender. West of Florence, in the hills of Artimino, the restaurant Da Delfina serves exceptional versions of local standards, such as this herbed rabbit. A Florentine note on cooking with wine: Never cook with a wine you wouldn't be happy to drink.

1 Rinse the rabbit pieces. Pat dry with paper towels. In a large, heavy-bottomed frying pan over medium heat, warm 3 tablespoons of the olive oil. Lay the rabbit pieces in a single layer in the pan and cook, using kitchen tongs to turn them, until lightly browned on all sides, about 10 minutes. Transfer the rabbit to a plate.

2 Add the remaining 3 tablespoons oil to the same pan over medium heat. Add the onions, celery, carrot, garlic, rosemary, sage, parsley, and bay leaves and cook, stirring frequently, until the vegetables are fragrant and tender, about 10 minutes.

3 Reduce the heat to medium-low, return the rabbit to the pan, and pour in the wine. Cook, stirring and turning the pieces occasionally and adding a bit of water to the pan if it is drying out, until the rabbit pieces are almost tender when pierced with a fork, about 1 hour.

4 Add ½ cup (4 fl oz/125 ml) water, the pine nuts, and the olives and stir well. Continue cooking until the rabbit has soaked up most of the liquid, about 20 minutes longer. Season with salt and pepper.

5 Divide the rabbit pieces among warmed individual plates. Top with the pine nuts, olives, and vegetables. Serve at once.

Serve with a bright, Sangiovese-based red wine such as Carmignano or a crisp white wine such as Vermentino.

1 rabbit, about 3½ lb (1.75 kg), cut into 8 serving pieces by the butcher

6 tablespoons (3 fl oz/90 ml) extra-virgin olive oil

2 yellow onions, finely chopped

2 celery stalks, finely chopped

1 large carrot, peeled and finely chopped

2 cloves garlic, minced

1 tablespoon finely chopped fresh rosemary

1 tablespoon finely chopped fresh sage

1 tablespoon finely chopped fresh flat-leaf (Italian) parsley

2 bay leaves

1 cup (8 fl oz/250 ml) dry white wine

1 cup (5 oz/155 g) pine nuts

¾ cup (3 oz/90 g) brine-cured pitted black olives

Salt and freshly ground pepper

Makes 4 servings

Alla Corte del Vino

A common lament among wine-loving visitors to Tuscany is "So much wine, so little time." Whatever the state of one's pocketbook or physiology, it seems impossible to taste all the outstanding wines of the region. During one weekend each May, however, the *principe* Corsini, from one of Florence's oldest noble families, opens the grounds, formal gardens, and courtyard of their stunning fifteenth-century Renaissance villa Le Corti for Alla Corte del Vino, a celebration of Tuscan wine and food.

This event presents a chance not only to taste the best wines from more than one hundred of Tuscany's finest winemakers, but also to attend seminars, ask questions, buy wines, and speak to the winemakers themselves. Italy's wine culture is an unusually unpretentious one. Winemakers are happy to pour wine and share conversation with the neophyte and knowledgeable alike. They chat amicably among themselves and taste one anothers' wines before ambling off to visit colleagues from other wineries. It's hard to imagine a nicer way to spend a Tuscan spring day.

COSTOLETTE D'AGNELLO AI PEPI

Lamb Chops with Mixed Peppercorns

The hilltown of San Casciano is only twenty minutes from Florence, yet it is a world apart, with its slower rhythms and pedestrian-only main road lined with bakeries, greengrocers, butchers, and wine shops. You will also find the Caffè del Popolano, whose candlelit tables spill out of two snug rooms onto the cobbled street. Farther down the road, the shop Ciappi sells spices out of tall glass jars, including the peppercorns that Popolano's chef, Stefano Terreni, uses on his lamb chops. "Tuscans tend to overcook lamb," he cautions. "Lamb chops are best pink and moist inside."

1 rack of lamb with 8 chops, about 2 lb (1 kg)

2 tablespoons mixed black, white, green, and pink peppercorns, lightly cracked

5 tablespoons (3 fl oz/80 ml) extra-virgin olive oil

1 yellow onion, minced

1 carrot, peeled and minced

1 celery stalk, minced

2 cloves garlic, minced

2 teaspoons finely chopped fresh rosemary

1½ cups (12 fl oz/375 ml) dry white wine

Salt and freshly ground pepper

Makes 4 servings

1 Trim the rack of lamb of all but a thin layer of surface fat. Set aside the trimmings and cut between the ribs to separate the chops. Rub each chop on both sides with the peppercorns and set aside.

2 In a saucepan over low heat, warm 3 tablespoons of the olive oil. Add the onion, carrot, celery, garlic, and rosemary and sauté, stirring often, until the vegetables are softened and fragrant but not browned, about 15 minutes. Raise the heat to high, add the reserved lamb trimmings, and cook, stirring often, until brown on all sides, about 5 minutes. Add 1 cup (8 fl oz/250 ml) of the wine to the pan and cook until the alcohol evaporates, about 3 minutes. Season to taste with salt and pepper, then reduce the heat to medium-low and add 3 cups (24 fl oz/750 ml) water. Cook until about 1 cup of the liquid has evaporated, about 30 minutes. Strain through a fine-mesh sieve and set aside. Discard the solids.

3 In a large frying pan over high heat, warm the remaining 2 tablespoons olive oil. Add the chops and cook until well browned on each side, about

6 minutes total. Pour in the remaining ½ cup (4 fl oz/ 125 ml) wine and cook until the alcohol has evaporated, about 2 minutes. Pour the reserved sauce over the chops and cook, turning once, 3–5 minutes per side. To test for doneness, make a small cut into one of the chops; it should still be pink inside. Remove the chops from the pan and set aside.

4 Raise the heat to high and cook the pan juices until they have reached a syrupy consistency, about 5 minutes. Divide the chops among warmed individual plates. Spoon the sauce over the chops and serve at once.

Serve with a well-structured red wine such as Vino Nobile di Montepulciano or a Super Tuscan made from 100 percent Sangiovese.

BACCALÀ ALLA FIORENTINA

Salt Cod, Florentine Style

In the hills just south of Florence lies Arcetri, home of some of the city's most beautiful villas. Despite its proximity to Florence, the place has an astonishingly bucolic feel. On an ancient cobbled road seemingly in the middle of nowhere is the lovely traditional Tuscan restaurant Omero. On Fridays, in keeping with the Catholic tradition of meatless Friday, it offers baccalà, *salt cod. "Buy only the best-quality salt cod," insists Omero's Roberto Viviani. "It should be white in color rather than yellow, with the skin still attached."*

1 Place the salt cod in a large bowl of cold water, cover, and refrigerate for 36–48 hours, changing the water every 6–8 hours.

2 Drain the cod and remove any skin and bones. Pat dry, cut into large pieces about 2½ by 5 inches (6 by 13 cm), and dredge with flour.

3 Pour olive oil to a depth of about ½ inch (12 mm) into a large frying pan and place over low heat. Add the garlic and sauté until golden, about 2 minutes. Remove and discard the garlic. Continue heating the oil until it is very hot but not smoking, about 2 minutes. Increase the heat to medium. Distribute the fish pieces in a single layer in the pan and cook, turning once, until they are opaque on both sides, about 6 minutes total. Transfer the fish to several layers of paper towels to drain and set aside.

4 Discard the oil in the frying pan, wipe it clean, add the 3 tablespoons olive oil, and place over medium heat. Add the tomatoes and parsley and cover with the fish in a single layer. Reduce the heat to medium-low and cook for 10 minutes, occasionally lifting the fish from the pan bottom with a spatula to keep it from sticking and spooning the tomatoes over it. Season to taste with pepper.

5 Divide the fish and sauce among warmed individual plates and serve at once.

Serve with an aged Chianti Classico or Vino Nobile di Montepulciano.

2 lb (1 kg) salt cod

All-purpose (plain) flour for dredging

3 tablespoons extra-virgin olive oil, plus more for frying

3 cloves garlic, crushed

2 cups (12 oz/375 g) canned crushed plum (Roma) tomatoes

1 tablespoon finely chopped fresh flat-leaf (Italian) parsley

Freshly ground pepper

Makes 6 servings

Salt Cod

Baccalà, salt cod, is a fixture on Friday menus throughout the city of Florence, in keeping with *il venerdì di magro,* the Catholic church's tradition of meatless Friday, which has become as much a gastronomic as a religious observance. The prevalence of salt cod in Florence harks back to the time when lack of refrigeration or rapid transport made access to fresh fish in inland cities nearly impossible. In the fifteenth century, whalers off the coast of Newfoundland learned to preserve precious Atlantic cod (*merluzzo,* in Italian) by salting it. They cleaned and salted the cod aboard the fishing boats, then dried it on land. By the 1600s, the Netherlands had become Europe's largest exporter of salt cod, and it remains so today.

In Florence, *baccalà* (not to be confused with *stoccafisso,* which is air-dried cod that is not salted) is found not only at fishmongers but also in many cheese shops, packed in plastic tubs surrounded by a layer of sea salt. The fish is rehydrated before cooking by soaking it in several changes of cold water over a period of 36 to 48 hours.

OSSOBUCO ALLA FIORENTINA

Osso Buco, Florentine Style

Located on Via delle Belle Donne (Street of the Beautiful Women) is a tiny osteria of the same name. The room is dominated by an enormous edible still life of pumpkins, cabbages, artichokes, tomatoes, fruits, or whatever the season offers. A blackboard propped against a corner lists the day's menu. A standard dish for more than fifteen years is chef Filippo Cianchi's ossobuco alla fiorentina, *his own version of the famous Milanese dish. It is much easier to make than the traditional dish, since it is not served with saffron risotto or garnished with* gremolata *(minced garlic, lemon zest, and parsley), but it is equally delicious.*

4 slices veal shank, each 1½–2 inches (4–5 cm) thick, with bone and marrow

Salt and freshly ground pepper

3 tablespoons extra-virgin olive oil

2 yellow onions, finely chopped

2 carrots, peeled and finely chopped

2 celery stalks, finely chopped

1 cup (8 fl oz/250 ml) dry red wine

3 canned plum (Roma) tomatoes, coarsely chopped

Makes 4 servings

1 Preheat the oven to 325°F (165°C). Score the outer edge of each veal shank at the meaty side of the shank opposite the bone with 2 shallow cuts about 2 inches (5 cm) apart, so the meat remains flat during cooking. Generously season with salt and pepper. In a frying pan over medium-high heat, warm the olive oil. Add the shanks and cook on the first side until golden brown, about 4 minutes. Turn the shanks and cook on the second side until browned, about 4 minutes longer. Transfer to a plate.

2 Reduce the heat to medium and add the onions, carrots, and celery to the pan. Sauté, adding a few tablespoons of water if the pan dries out, until the vegetables are softened, about 10 minutes. Add the wine, raise the heat to high, and cook until the alcohol evaporates, about 3 minutes. Remove from the heat and stir in the tomatoes.

3 Lightly oil a roasting pan large enough to hold the shanks comfortably. Transfer the shanks to the pan. Spoon the vegetable mixture over the meat, cover with aluminum foil, and cook until the veal is fork-tender, about 1½ hours.

4 Transfer the veal to warmed individual plates. Spoon the pan juices over the top and serve.

Serve with a robust, full-bodied red wine such as a Tuscan Cabernet Sauvignon.

CONTORNI

Contorni, the vegetable side dishes of Italy, change with the seasons,

offering refreshing or warming counterparts to meat-based main dishes.

Roasted potatoes, white beans smothered in tomato sauce, and greens dressed in lemon juice are Florence's most ubiquitous *contorni*. These delicious elaborations are governed by the cycle of seasons. In spring there will be artichokes and fresh peas cooked with onion or pancetta. Summer brings grilled eggplant (aubergine), braised red and yellow bell peppers (capsicums), green beans stewed with plum (Roma) tomatoes, and zucchini (courgettes) sautéed with garlic, fresh parsley, and olive oil. Autumn is the time for porcino mushrooms, and winter for Tuscany's famed deep green *cavolo nero,* or black cabbage.

PEPERONATA

Braised Sweet Peppers, Tomatoes, and Onions

Just across from the Mercato di Sant'Ambrogio is a tiny restaurant named after its owner, Gilda. It's a charming place with mismatched glasses and chairs and snippets of poetry in the menu, perfect for lunch after a morning of marketing. This side dish from Gilda is a summer gem, as bright and colorful on the palate as it is on the plate. Peperonata *is braised on the stove top to bring out the innate sweetness of all its ingredients. A quintessential warm-weather dish, it pairs well with panfried chicken or veal* scaloppine.

1 Cut the bell peppers into 2-inch (5-cm) squares. In a saucepan over low heat, combine the peppers, olive oil, onion, and bay leaves and cook, stirring often, until the vegetables are softened and have released their juices, about 15 minutes.

2 Add the tomatoes, season to taste with salt and pepper, and simmer gently until the vegetables are soft, about 5 minutes. Remove and discard the bay leaves. Serve the *peperonata* warm or chilled.

Note: The success of this dish largely depends on using ripe, seasonal tomatoes. If ripe tomatoes are unavailable, substitute canned whole plum (Roma) tomatoes.

1 lb (500 g) red bell peppers (capsicums), stems, ribs, and seeds removed

¼ cup (2 fl oz/60 ml) extra-virgin olive oil

1 red onion, halved and thinly sliced crosswise

2 bay leaves

3 tomatoes, peeled and seeded (page 187), then coarsely chopped

Salt and freshly ground pepper

Makes 4 servings

Tuesdays at Le Cascine

Almost every town in Tuscany has its own market day, and Florence is no exception. Every Tuesday morning, Le Cascine park is transformed into a giant open-air *mercato* with vendors selling everything from fruits and vegetables to kitchen gadgets, housewares, clothing, pets, linens, and cleaning products—often at prices considerably lower than those found elsewhere.

Le Cascine, a true working market used by locals, seems to go on forever. Vendors come from all of Italy to sell their wares. A man from Apulia sits on a stool with a handheld scale selling nothing but cherries. Another has driven from Calabria with crates of bright red and yellow peppers. A farmer whose hand-painted sign says *cultivatore diretto di Scandicci* (meaning his products come from his farm in the countryside) stands behind a table heaped with fresh produce. There is a vendor who sells only bee products, another who specializes in vegetables preserved in olive oil or vinegar. Completing the Italian kaleidoscope are olives of every persuasion, dried fruits, nuts, and spices, as well as many cheeses and cured meats.

ASPARAGI CON UOVO E PARMIGIANO

Asparagus with Fried Eggs and Parmesan

Apple green bunches of asparagus in various thicknesses are one of the first signs that winter has finally given way to primavera, or spring. The thinnest asparagus spears are gathered wild in the countryside, their scarcity and brief seasonality translating into a relatively high price tag. Wild asparagus is a prized ingredient in frittatas and the occasional pasta sauce. Thick-stalked cultivated asparagus is used for this dish, which, though meatless, is considered substantial enough to be offered as a main course in some Florentine restaurants. Serve with a salad of baby lettuces and country bread.

20 medium- to thick-stalked asparagus spears, about 1 lb (500 g) total weight

2 tablespoons butter

4 extra-large eggs, preferably organic

Salt and freshly ground pepper

½ cup (2 oz/60 g) freshly grated Parmigiano-Reggiano cheese

Makes 4 servings

1 Bring a large pot three-fourths full of water to a boil. Cut or snap off the tough end from each asparagus spear. Use a vegetable peeler to pare away the tough outer skin of each spear to within about 2 inches (5 cm) of the tip.

2 Divide the asparagus spears into 4 equal bunches and tie each bunch at the base with kitchen string. Add the asparagus bundles, tips up, to the boiling water and cook until the spears are tender but still firm, 4–6 minutes. Drain well, remove the strings, and arrange the spears on individual plates.

3 In a large frying pan over medium heat, melt the butter. Break each egg into the pan, taking care not to puncture the yolk or let the egg whites overlap.

Cook for 2 minutes, then season with salt and pepper. Sprinkle 2 tablespoons water into the pan, cover, and cook until the whites are solid but the yolks are still runny, about 2 minutes. Using a spatula, carefully drape 1 fried egg over each serving of asparagus. Sprinkle liberally with the Parmigiano-Reggiano and serve.

Serve with a violet-scented red wine such as Rosso di Montepulciano or a creamy white wine such as a Tuscan Chardonnay.

ZUCCHINI TRIFOLATI

Zucchini with Olive Oil, Garlic, and Parsley

Although Florentines like their pasta al dente, the trend of cooking vegetables only briefly so they retain their color and texture has been greeted with little enthusiasm. Florentines prefer their vegetables well cooked and flavored. Those cooked with the delicious trinity of olive oil, garlic, and parsley are described as trifolati. *Mushrooms and zucchini are two of the best vegetables to cook this way. They not only make a flavorful side dish but are delicious as a pasta sauce as well.*

1 Trim the stem ends of each zucchini. Cut in half lengthwise and then cut crosswise into slices about ⅜ inch (1 cm) thick.

2 In a large, heavy-bottomed frying pan over medium heat, warm the olive oil. Add the garlic and sauté until fragrant and golden, about 2 minutes. Add the zucchini and sauté, stirring often, until the zucchini are quite soft, 15–20 minutes. Sprinkle the parsley over the zucchini toward the end of the cooking time. Season to taste with salt and pepper and serve.

2 lb (1 kg) zucchini (courgettes)

⅓ cup (3 fl oz/80 ml) extra-virgin olive oil

2 cloves garlic, finely chopped

2 tablespoons finely chopped fresh flat-leaf (Italian) parsley

Salt and freshly ground pepper

Makes 4 servings

Tuscan Kitchenware

La cucina is the obvious heart of most Florentine homes. What it may lack in sophisticated appliances (generally deemed frivolous) it makes up for in charm and functionality. Cupboards are filled with well-loved pieces of majolica from the nearby town of Montelupo Fiorentino or perhaps with fine Florentine porcelain from Richard Ginori. You will almost always find stacks of crisply ironed table linens and *canovacci* (tea towels), as well as a wide assortment of hardworking, hands-on kitchen tools.

Florence seems to inspire visitors to create their own Italian kitchens at home. It's easy enough to do—the city is a shopper's paradise. The stock at Bartolini on Via dei Servi, an excellent place to start, ranges from the lowliest stove-top espresso makers to fire engine red antique meat slicers to fine china. Visit the tiny Luca della Robbia majolica shop on Via del Proconsolo for ceramics. Expect to find owner Michele Cantarutti seated in front of an easel, working away on an oil painting while you happily shop for traditional Florentine majolica, much of which has been hand-painted at his family's factory in Montelupo Fiorentino.

FAGIOLI ALL'UCCELLETTO

White Beans in Tomato Sauce

White beans—usually cannellini—are to Tuscany what borlotti beans are to northern Italy. In fact, Tuscans have such a reputation for eating beans that they are sometimes referred to by other Italians as mangia-fagioli, or bean eaters. The most basic preparation for white beans is simply stewed with garlic and sage, with the finished beans always served with a generous drizzling of extra-virgin olive oil. When cooked all'uccelletto (in the manner of little birds), they are flavored with tomatoes and scented with sage, and they are the preferred accompaniment to grilled sausages, bistecche, and other meats.

2 cups (1 lb/500 g) dried cannellini beans (page 185)

¼ cup (2 fl oz/60 ml) plus 2 tablespoons extra-virgin olive oil

4 cloves garlic, crushed, plus 2 cloves garlic, unpeeled

4 or 5 fresh sage leaves, plus 1 fresh sage sprig

3 or 4 peppercorns

Salt and freshly ground pepper

1½ cups (9 oz/280 g) canned whole plum (Roma) tomatoes

Makes 4 servings

1 Pick over the beans, discarding any grit or misshapen beans. Rinse well, place in a large bowl, and add cold water to cover generously. Let soak overnight.

2 The next day, drain the beans, then rinse well and place them in a heavy soup pot. Add 8 cups (64 fl oz/ 2 l) water, the 2 tablespoons olive oil, the unpeeled garlic, the sage leaves, and the peppercorns, cover, and bring to a simmer over medium heat. Reduce the heat so that the water simmers very gently and cook until the skins of the beans are tender and the interiors are soft, 1½–2 hours. Season to taste with salt three-fourths of the way through the cooking time.

3 Drain the beans, reserving the liquid. Remove and discard the unpeeled garlic. In a large, heavy-bottomed frying pan over medium heat, warm the ¼ cup olive oil. Add the crushed garlic and sauté until fragrant and golden, about 3 minutes. Add the tomatoes, crushing and breaking them apart with a wooden spoon. Add the sage sprig and season to taste with salt and pepper. Let simmer until a thick sauce forms, about 20 minutes. Add the beans and 1 cup (8 fl oz/250 ml) of their cooking liquid. Taste and adjust the seasoning. Return to a simmer and cook gently, stirring occasionally, until the sauce has thickened to a medium consistency, about 15 minutes.

4 Remove and discard the sage sprig. Transfer to a shallow platter and serve.

PISELLI SGRANATI CON CIPOLLA E BASILICO

Freshly Shucked Peas with Onion and Basil

Fresh peas are one example of the premium Florentines put on seasonal ingredients. For most of the year, piselli *tend to be absent from menus and markets. In springtime, however, they abound. They are sold still in their pods, heaped in baskets at farmers' markets and the* fruttivendolo *(greengrocer). Some greengrocers sell small quantities of peas that they have shucked while passing the time between customers. If you find fresh peas on a menu, expect to pay for them—they are worth the price.*

1 Shell the peas into a bowl and set aside. You should have about 4 cups (1¼ lb/625 g) shelled peas.

2 In a heavy-bottomed saucepan over low heat, warm the olive oil. Add the onion and sauté until softened and translucent but not browned, about 10 minutes. Add the peas and stir well. Pour in just enough water to cover the peas, cover the pan, and cook until soft but not mushy, 7–10 minutes. Add the sugar, season to taste with salt and pepper, and stir in the basil. Continue cooking until the peas are tender but still firm, about 5 minutes longer. Transfer to a serving dish and serve.

4 lb (2 kg) spring peas in their pods

6 tablespoons (3 fl oz/90 ml) extra-virgin olive oil

1 yellow onion, chopped

1 teaspoon sugar

Salt and freshly ground pepper

Handful of fresh basil leaves

Makes 4 servings

La Fierucola

Florence's *fierucola* in Piazza Santo Spirito and *fierucolina* in Piazza Santissima Annunziata are organic farmers' markets. The former is held on the third Sunday of the month, the latter on the first Saturday. Both are inspired by a historical tradition whereby farmers and their families lit lanterns and walked in procession to Piazza Santissima Annunziata to celebrate the birth of the Virgin Mary. The following day, the square became a fairground, with farmers selling hand-carded wool, dried mushrooms, berries, cheese, and other products from their farms and the surrounding woodlands.

Today's *fierucola* is famous for products like handmade cheeses, dark loaves of bread, and raspberry jam sweetened with wild honey. "This is a market with an ethic," explains Giannozzo Pucci, one of the handful of people responsible for bringing *la fierucola* back to life, "an ethic of supporting those farmers who not only operate without pesticides and chemical fertilizers, but who also use their land responsibly, in a way that enriches rather than depletes it."

CARCIOFI E PATATE BRASATI

Braised Artichokes and Potatoes

Next to tomatoes, artichokes are perhaps Florence's favorite vegetable. At one extreme are the mamme, *large globelike artichokes that are usually boiled and eaten with olive oil and lemon juice. At the other are the tiny, smooth-leaved* morellini, *whose tenderness and undeveloped chokes make them best for eating raw in salads. Somewhere in between are the relatively small, tough-leaved* carciofi, *often sold still on their thick stalks. When cleaned down to their tender leaves and hearts, they are cut into wedges and served in a variety of ways, the following being a Florentine favorite.*

Juice of 1 lemon

4 artichokes, about 1 lb (500 g) total weight

¼ cup (2 fl oz/60 ml) extra-virgin olive oil

2 yellow onions, chopped

1½ lb (750 g) new potatoes, cut into chunks

Leaves of 1 fresh thyme sprig

Salt and freshly ground pepper

Makes 4 servings

1 Add the lemon juice to a bowl of cold water. Working with 1 artichoke at a time, pull off the outer leaves until you reach the pale, tender inner leaves. Using a knife, cut off the tough green tops of the leaves until only the tender, edible portion remains. Trim the stem to 1 inch (2.5 cm) and pare away the tough outer layer. Cut each artichoke in half lengthwise and use a spoon to remove the hairy choke. Cut each artichoke half into 4 wedges and place in the bowl of lemon water until ready to use.

2 In a heavy-bottomed soup pot over medium heat, warm the olive oil. Add the onions and sauté until golden and fragrant, about 8 minutes. Add the potatoes and sauté until lightly colored on all sides, about 15 minutes. Reduce the heat to low. Drain the artichokes and add to the pot with the thyme leaves and 1 cup (8 fl oz/250 ml) water. Season to taste with salt and pepper. Cover and cook, stirring occasionally and adding water as necessary to keep the pan from drying out, until the potatoes are cooked through and the artichokes are soft, about 15 minutes. Transfer to a shallow bowl and serve.

SPINACI ALL'AGRO
Spinach with Lemon and Olive Oil

Citrus trees are unable to withstand Tuscan winters, when nighttime temperatures often drop to freezing. In the grandest villas, lemon trees are planted in terra-cotta pots and moved into splendid limonaie, or citrus conservatories, to wait out the winter. Then lemons must be brought in from Sicily and the south, where the climate remains more temperate. Florentines often prefer lemon juice to vinegar (which in their opinion ruins the palate for wine), and like to dress both salads and cooked greens with olive oil, lemon juice, and salt.

1 Put the spinach with just the rinsing water clinging to the leaves in a heavy-bottomed soup pot over medium heat. Cook, covered, until soft and wilted, about 5 minutes. Drain well in a colander, pressing against the spinach with a wooden spoon to extract as much water as possible.

2 Transfer the spinach to a serving bowl. Add the olive oil and lemon juice and toss to combine. Season to taste with salt and serve at once.

2 bunches spinach, about 2 lb (1 kg) total weight, tough stems removed

3 tablespoons extra-virgin olive oil

Juice of ½ lemon

Salt

Makes 4 servings

Cooked Greens

Cooked greens of some kind are among the most common and traditional Florentine side dishes and are offered as a *contorno* on the menus of virtually every local trattoria. *Spinaci* is a favorite, although it is rather labor-intensive to clean and prepare for cooking. A sink full of spinach cooks down to a mere four or five portions. Sturdier Swiss chard can easily be rinsed, trimmed, chopped, and sautéed in olive oil.

Turnip greens *(cime di rapa)* and a relative, broccoli rabe *(rapini* or *broccoli di rape),* satisfy the Florentine love of *l'agro,* which translates as sharp, bitter, sour, or tart. Though related to turnips, broccoli rabe differs considerably in appearance. At the ends of its leafy green stems are clusters of broccoli-like florets.

Spinach, chard, and *rapini* are often available precooked in tight round balls at some greengrocers and at the same shops that sell cured meats, cheeses, olives, and the like, for quick sautéing and dressing with fruity olive oil. They are seasoned with salt and—if they haven't been sautéed in garlic—a splash of freshly squeezed lemon juice.

DOLCI

Never overly sweet or complicated, desserts in Florence are usually simple—

often a sampling of the season's freshest fruit or a modest baked treat.

A dish of wild strawberries sprinkled with sugar, peaches soaked in white wine, roasted chestnuts, or a ripe persimmon tends to delight a Florentine more than an elaborate confection. A plate of pale, hard "twice-baked" biscotti flavored with almonds and citrus zest and a small glass of sweet, amber *vin santo* are offered for dipping at most local trattorias. Locals and visitors alike can be seen walking the streets eating gelati and *sorbetti* (sorbets) from one of the city's many *gelaterie.* Baked desserts tend to be homey and simple, though a custard-filled *crostata di frutta* looks and tastes elegant enough to satisfy any dessert lover's sweet tooth.

SORBETTO DI PESCA

Peach Sorbet

Peaches are a favorite summer fruit in Tuscany, where they are often sliced into a pitcher of chilled white wine and left to soak for a couple of hours before serving for dessert. The appeal of sorbetto is that it is little more than the fruit itself—the fresher and riper the fruit, the better. Pesca (peach), fragola (strawberry), and limone (lemon) are popular sorbet flavors throughout Florence, but keep your eyes out as well for unexpected sorbets like fig, blood orange, persimmon, and Concord grape.

1 Bring a large saucepan three-fourths full of water to a boil. Score a shallow X on the blossom end of each peach. Slip 2 peaches at a time into the boiling water and blanch for about 30 seconds. Using a slotted spoon, remove the peaches from the water and set aside. When they are cool enough to handle, peel away the skins. Cut the peeled peaches from the pits. In a blender or food processor, purée the peaches until smooth. Transfer the peach purée to a bowl, cover, and refrigerate until well chilled, about 3 hours.

2 Meanwhile, in a small saucepan over medium heat, combine 3 cups (24 fl oz/750 ml) water and the sugar and bring to a boil. Reduce the heat to low and simmer until the sugar has dissolved, about 4 minutes. Remove the sugar syrup from the heat and let cool, then stir it into the chilled peach purée. Add the lemon juice, stir well to combine, and return the bowl to the refrigerator for 1 hour.

3 Pour the mixture into an ice-cream maker and freeze according to the manufacturer's instructions. Unless your ice-cream maker has a built-in freezing compartment, transfer the sorbet to a freezer-safe container. Cover and freeze the sorbet until firm, at least 3 hours or up to 3 days, before serving.

Serve with a peachy, melon-scented sparkling white wine such as Prosecco.

6 peaches, about 3 lb (1.5 kg) total weight

1⅓ cups (11 oz/345 g) sugar

Juice of ½ lemon

Makes 8 servings

Sorbetti

During Italy's torrid Mediterranean summers, nothing is more refreshing than an icy and sweet *sorbetto,* or sorbet. *Sorbetti* are sold in *gelaterie* and are recognizable by their bright colors: *fragola* (strawberry), the color of roses; the deep burgundy of *frutti di bosco* (woodland berries); and the lively yellow of tart *limone.* They are water based, making them lighter in texture and easier to digest than gelati, which use a base of milk or cream. *Sorbetti* are most often made with fresh fruit, but creative cooks also flavor them with herbs and edible flowers such as mint and verbena.

Italian *sorbetti* were first made in Sicily, under Arab tutelage, using fresh fruits, honey, and snow from Mount Etna, which was collected during winter and stored in basements up to one hundred feet (40 m) deep. By the sixteenth century, *sorbetto* was regularly served between courses of a meal as a palate refresher in Catherine de' Medici's Florentine court. Ultimately she brought *sorbetto* to Paris, where it became known by the French word *sorbet.*

GELATO DI CREMA AL PROFUMO DI CAFFÈ

Coffee-Scented Custard Gelato

The basic gelato flavor in Tuscany is not vanilla but crema, *made with deep orange egg yolks and milk rather than cream. This quintessential flavor can be lightly scented using coffee beans, as below; vanilla beans; lemon or orange zest; or even a splash of* vin santo. *Gelato is soft and malleable, more suited for a spatula than a metal ice-cream scoop. Serve this gelato to friends after a summer lunch or dinner, followed by a bracing cup of espresso. Or, serve the gelato with the espresso poured over the top, a favorite Italian treat called* affogato al caffè *(drowned ice cream).*

4 cups (32 fl oz/1 l) whole milk

1 cup (8 oz/250 g) sugar

15 dark-roasted coffee beans

Pinch of salt

6 large egg yolks, lightly beaten

Makes 8 servings

1 Have ready a large bowl partially filled with ice cubes and water. In a heavy-bottomed saucepan over medium heat, combine the milk, ½ cup (4 oz/125 g) of the sugar, the coffee beans, and the salt. Cook until small bubbles appear along the edges of the pan, about 5 minutes.

2 Meanwhile, in a bowl, combine the egg yolks with the remaining ½ cup sugar. Whisk until very thick and pale yellow. Whisking constantly, slowly add about ½ cup (4 fl oz/125 ml) of the warm milk mixture to the egg mixture. Return the egg mixture to the remaining milk mixture in the saucepan and cook over medium heat, stirring constantly with a wooden spoon, until it is thick enough to coat the back of the spoon and leaves a clear trail when a finger is drawn through it, 5–7 minutes. Do not let boil. Remove from the heat and place the saucepan in the bowl of ice water to stop the cooking. Stir occasionally to facilitate cooling.

3 When the custard reaches room temperature, cover with plastic wrap, pressing it directly onto the surface to prevent a skin from forming. Refrigerate until well chilled, at least 2 hours or up to 12 hours.

4 Strain the custard through a medium-mesh sieve into a bowl. Discard the coffee beans. Transfer the mixture to an ice-cream maker and freeze according to the manufacturer's instructions. Unless your ice-cream maker has a built-in freezing compartment, transfer the gelato to a freezer-safe container. Cover and freeze the gelato until firm, at least 3 hours or up to 3 days, before serving.

CROSTATA DI LAMPONI
Raspberry Tart

Piazza Beccaria's pastry shop Dolci & Dolcezze has a storybook charm to it. Gilded doors open onto chandelier-lit walls lacquered a pale, soothing green. Behind spotless glass cases are arguably the city's most delicious tarts, pies, and puddings. Giulio Corti makes his fruit tarts with pasta frolla—short-crust pastry—and sells them both in large pies that serve eight and in small, individual tarts to eat standing up at the small bar with a frothy cappuccino or a glass of iced Lapsang souchong tea. This tart is beautiful to behold, whether you choose the uniform look of all raspberries or a mix of any fresh berries in season.

1 To make the crust, in a large bowl, use a wooden spoon to combine the butter, egg, and granulated sugar. Add the flour and mix with the wooden spoon until a homogenous dough forms. Roll into a ball, cover with plastic wrap, and refrigerate for at least 2 hours or up to 8 hours.

2 Preheat the oven to 400°F (200°C). Butter a 9½-inch (24-cm) tart pan with a removable bottom and preferably with straight sides. Unwrap the refrigerated dough and place on a lightly floured work surface. Using a lightly floured rolling pin, roll the dough out into a round ¹⁄₁₆–⅛ inch (2–3 mm) thick. Separate the tart pan bottom from the sides. Lay the dough round over the bottom, then trim the overhanging dough. Replace the dough-lined bottom into the pan sides. Gather up the dough scraps and roll into a rope about as thick as a finger. Lay the rope along the inside edge of the pan and press it into the bottom and up the sides of the pan to a height of ¾ inch (2 cm). If desired, create a zigzag edge by using a knife to cut the dough so that its edges form triangular points.

3 Line the tart shell with a piece of aluminum foil. Fill with a generous layer of dried beans or pie weights and bake until pale and dry, about 30 minutes. Remove the beans and foil, then return the crust to the oven and bake until golden, about 5 minutes longer. Transfer to a wire rack to cool. Carefully remove the crust from the tart pan and transfer to a serving plate.

4 To make the custard, in a heavy saucepan over medium heat, warm the milk until small bubbles appear along the edges of the pan, about 5 minutes.

5 Meanwhile, in a bowl, combine the egg yolks, granulated sugar, and cornstarch. Whisk until pale and creamy. Whisking constantly, slowly add about ½ cup (4 fl oz/125 ml) of the warm milk to the egg mixture. Return the egg mixture to the remaining milk in the saucepan and cook, whisking constantly, until the mixture thickens and begins to bubble around the edges of the pan, 5–8 minutes. Remove from the heat and continue stirring for 1 minute longer. Pour the custard though a medium-mesh sieve into a bowl. Let cool slightly, stirring occasionally, then pour the custard into the tart crust, using a rubber spatula to distribute it evenly.

6 When the custard has cooled completely, arrange the raspberries on top in a single layer. Dust lightly with confectioners' sugar and serve.

Serve with a sweet, fragrant white dessert wine such as *vin santo.*

FOR THE CRUST

¾ cup (6 oz/185 g) unsalted butter, at room temperature

1 large egg, lightly beaten

⅓ cup (3 oz/90 g) granulated sugar

2 cups (8 oz/250 g) cake (soft-wheat) flour

FOR THE CUSTARD

3 cups (24 fl oz/750 ml) whole milk

8 large egg yolks

¾ cup (6 oz/185 g) granulated sugar

¼ cup (1 oz/30 g) cornstarch (cornflour)

2 cups (8 oz/250 g) raspberries or other fresh berries, such as blackberries, hulled strawberries, or blueberries

Confectioners' (icing) sugar for dusting

Makes one 9½-inch (24-cm) tart

TORTA DI MELE CON CREMA ALL'INGLESE
Apple Torte with Custard Cream

Every so often, one stumbles into a café so charmingly homey and welcoming that the day's plans go out the window, replaced by the simple desire to pull up a chair and while away the hours with a good book, a pot of tea or bowl of caffellatte, and a slice of homemade cake. Vanna Casati Gnot's Caffellatte is that sort of place: mismatched chairs, wildflowers in jam jars, a lovely range of fine teas (from semifermented oolong to Rooibos), coffee, and a selection of wonderful homemade cakes, including this apple torte. Grated lemon zest adds a twist to the custard cream that is served alongside.

FOR THE TORTE

2½ cups (10 oz/315 g) cake (soft-wheat) flour

1 teaspoon baking powder

4 large eggs

½ cup (4 oz/125 g) sugar

2 tablespoons extra-virgin olive oil

2 tablespoons whole milk

1 teaspoon vanilla extract (essence)

1½ lb (750 g) cooking apples, such as McIntosh or Rome Beauty, peeled, cored, and cut into small chunks

FOR THE CUSTARD CREAM

2½ cups (20 fl oz/625 ml) whole milk

3 large egg yolks

¼ cup (2 oz/60 g) sugar

Grated zest of ½ lemon

Makes one 9-inch (23-cm) torte

1 Preheat the oven to 350°F (180°C). Oil and lightly flour a 9-inch (23-cm) springform pan.

2 Sift the flour and baking powder into a bowl. In a separate bowl, beat the eggs and sugar together until pale and creamy. Add the olive oil, milk, and vanilla and stir well to combine. Use a wooden spoon to incorporate the flour mixture gradually into the egg mixture, stirring to form a thick batter. Stir in the apple chunks and pour into the prepared pan. Bake until a toothpick inserted into the center of the torte comes out clean, 50–60 minutes. Transfer to a wire rack, remove the sides of the pan, and let cool.

3 To make the custard cream, in a heavy-bottomed saucepan over medium heat, heat the milk until small bubbles appear along the edges of the pan, about 5 minutes.

4 Meanwhile, in a nonreactive bowl, combine the egg yolks, sugar, and lemon zest. Whisk until pale and creamy. Whisking constantly, slowly add about ½ cup (4 fl oz/125 ml) of the warm milk to the egg mixture. Return the egg mixture to the remaining milk in the saucepan and cook, stirring constantly with a wooden spoon, until the mixture is thick enough to coat the back of the spoon and leaves a clear trail when a finger is drawn through it, 5–7 minutes. Do not let boil. Remove the custard cream from the heat and continue stirring for 2 minutes. Strain through a fine-mesh sieve into a bowl. If chilling the custard cream, cover with plastic wrap, pressing it directly onto the surface to prevent a skin from forming, and refrigerate for at least 2 hours or for up to 2 days.

5 Transfer the torte to a serving plate. Cut into slices and serve warm or cold, topping each slice with a small amount of warm or cold custard cream.

Serve with a pot of freshly brewed tea.

TORTA DI FICHI E NOCI

Fig and Walnut Torte

Some of the best food in Florence can be had at some of the least assuming places. The tiny Al Tranvai in Piazza Tasso, with its handful of indoor tables and a few more outside along the square, is one such gem. Owner Nanda Calamandrei's welcome is so direct and unpretentious, and her cooking so delightfully honest, that locals and travelers alike find themselves returning to Tranvai over and over again. Nanda's fig and walnut torte is a joy in a city not generally famous for its desserts.

1 Preheat the oven to 350°F (180°C). Butter a 9-inch (23-cm) springform pan.

2 In a small bowl, combine the figs and chopped walnuts and stir to combine. Distribute the fig and walnut mixture evenly in the bottom of the prepared pan and set aside.

3 In a large bowl, beat the eggs with the sugar until pale and creamy. Stir in the melted butter and vanilla. Sift the flour and baking powder into another bowl. Use a wooden spoon to incorporate the flour mixture gradually into the egg mixture, stirring to form a thick batter. Stir in the fennel seeds. Pour the batter over the fig and walnut mixture. Bake until a toothpick inserted into the center of the torte comes out clean, about 30 minutes.

4 Transfer to a wire rack and remove the sides of the pan. Let cool for 20 minutes. Garnish the top of the torte with the walnut halves, pushing them slightly into the torte so that they stand up on their sides. Let cool completely before serving.

Serve with *alkermes* (see right) or a sweet white dessert wine such as *vin santo.*

1 cup (5 oz/155 g) dried figs, coarsely chopped

½ cup (2 oz/60 g) chopped walnuts, plus ½ cup (2 oz/60 g) walnut halves

4 large eggs, well beaten

⅓ cup (3 oz/90 g) plus 2 tablespoons sugar

7 tablespoons (3½ oz/105 g) unsalted butter, melted and cooled

1 teaspoon vanilla extract (essence)

¾ cup (4 oz/125 g) all-purpose (plain) flour

1½ teaspoons baking powder

1 teaspoon fennel seeds

Makes one 9-inch (23-cm) torte

L'Officina Profumo Farmaceutica di Santa Maria Novella

The lettering over the door on number 16 Via della Scala gives hardly a hint of the wonders inside. You enter a dim marble corridor, leaving the bright bustle of the city behind. There is a musky sweetness in the air, earthy and ancient, as if the whole of the Tuscan countryside had been distilled into a scent that then seeped into the very soul of this place. This is L'Officina Profumo Farmaceutica di Santa Maria Novella.

Founded in the thirteenth century by the Dominican fathers of Santa Maria Novella, L'Officina has a main room that was once a church, with frescoed vaulted ceilings and rose windows. A wooden cabinet along one wall holds slender bottles of liqueurs and elixirs, the most famous of which is the quintessentially Florentine *alkermes,* flavored with cardamom, cloves, cinnamon, coriander, and dried cochineals, a kind of insect that colors the liqueur a vivid crimson. There are also honeys, fruit compotes, tisanes, natural herbal remedies, beautifully boxed soaps, and potpourri.

CIOCCOLATA CALDA CON PANNA MONTATA

Thick Hot Chocolate with Whipped Cream

Florentine hot chocolate is so decadently rich and dense that one could easily be convinced that it was made from little other than the finest melted dark chocolate. Arrowroot, a thickener similar to cornstarch (cornflour) but with a more neutral flavor, is actually the secret to its thickness. There are few greater pleasures on a cold winter day than sipping a cioccolata calda *in a place like the elegant café Rivoire in Piazza della Signoria. Rivoire arguably makes the best version in the city; it also sells small bags of its cocoa powder for those who want to attempt such delectability at home.*

FOR THE HOT CHOCOLATE

¾ cup (2½ oz/75 g) unsweetened cocoa powder

⅓ cup (3 oz/90 g) granulated sugar

3 cups (24 fl oz/750 ml) whole milk

1½ teaspoons arrowroot

½ cup (4 fl oz/125 ml) cold water

FOR THE WHIPPED CREAM

¾ cup (6 fl oz/180 ml) heavy (double) cream, well chilled

1½ teaspoons confectioners' (icing) sugar, sifted

Makes 6 servings

1 To make the hot chocolate, in a heavy-bottomed saucepan, whisk together the cocoa powder and granulated sugar. Place the saucepan over low heat and vigorously stir in ½ cup (4 fl oz/125 ml) of the milk, a few tablespoons at a time. When the mixture is smooth (with no lumps), stir in the remaining 2½ cups (20 fl oz/625 ml) milk. Bring to a boil over medium heat, stirring constantly. Reduce the heat to low and simmer, stirring often, for 5 minutes. Remove from the heat and let cool for 5 minutes.

2 Return the hot chocolate to a boil over medium heat, then reduce the heat to low and simmer for 5 minutes. Remove from the heat and let cool slightly.

3 In a small bowl, dissolve the arrowroot in the cold water. Pour into the hot chocolate. Bring to a boil over medium heat one final time, stirring constantly, then remove from the heat.

4 To make the whipped cream, in a bowl, combine the cream and confectioners' sugar. Using a wire whisk or electric mixer, beat until the cream is light and fluffy and holds soft peaks, about 4 minutes.

5 Pour the hot chocolate into teacups or mugs, top with the whipped cream, and serve at once.

MACEDONIA DI FRUTTA

Fruit Salad

Truth be told, Florentines do not have the sweet tooth of the English or the French or, for that matter, even their Italian neighbors to the north or the south. Give them the freshest whole fruit on a plate and a table knife to cut it with, and they will be happy. When fruits are made into a dessert, it is usually with a light hand: fragoline di bosco, *tiny woodland strawberries with a splash of fresh cream;* pesche al vino, *peaches in wine; or a seasonal* macedonia di frutta, *fruit salad dressed with lemon and sugar.*

1 Bring a saucepan three-fourths full of water to a boil. Score a shallow X on the blossom end of each peach. Slip the peaches into the boiling water and blanch for about 30 seconds. Using a slotted spoon, remove the peaches from the water and set aside.

2 Pour the lemon juice into a chilled serving bowl. Cut the watermelon and cantaloupe into 1-inch (2.5-cm) chunks directly over the bowl to capture all the juices.

3 Peel and core the apples and pears, cut them into ½-inch (12-mm) chunks, and transfer to the bowl.

4 Peel away the skins from the reserved peaches, then halve and remove the pits. Cut each half into ½-inch chunks directly over the bowl to capture all the juices. Halve the apricots, if using, and remove the pits. Cut into ½-inch chunks directly over the bowl.

5 Cut a slice off the top and bottom of one of the oranges, then stand it upright. Following the contour of the fruit, slice off the peel and white pith in thick strips. Holding the orange over a separate small bowl, cut along both sides of each segment to separate it from the membrane, letting each freed segment and any juices fall into the bowl. Repeat with the remaining orange. Cut the segments into ½-inch chunks directly over the bowl with the other fruit and add any juices remaining in the small bowl.

6 Sprinkle the fruit with the sugar and toss gently. Cover and refrigerate until well chilled, at least 1 hour or up to 8 hours, before serving.

2 firm yet ripe peaches

Juice of 2 lemons

1 slice whole watermelon, about 2 inches (5 cm) thick

½ ripe cantaloupe, peeled

2 ripe green apples such as Granny Smith

2 firm yet ripe pears

4 apricots (optional)

2 oranges

3 tablespoons sugar

Makes 6 servings

Cocomero

During the warm-weather months, fruit stands sprout up all around Florence—in the little square beside the *posta centrale* (main post office), at the edge of Le Cascine park, and along many of the main roads leading into the city. These are not the vendors from southern Italy who make their way up the country's slender boot with cargoes of fresh picked oranges or cherries to sell from trucks on the roadside, but are proper little mobile shops selling cold drinks, wedges of fresh coconut, and Florentines' favorite summer treat: *cocomero* (watermelon).

Thick, juicy wedges of watermelon are sold at the counter of these stands to be eaten *in piedi* (standing up). Behind the counter is a long table heaped with heavy, oval melons with rinds that are streaked a greenish gray. A few are cut in half, both to accommodate buyers who can't squeeze a whole melon into their small refrigerators and to entice those who can with the moist, red interiors dotted with shiny black seeds. Seedless watermelons have not had the success in Italy that they've had elsewhere—apparently Florentines like their fruits the way nature intended them.

BISCOTTINI DI PRATO

Almond Biscotti

Although they originated in the prosperous textile town of Prato, just northwest of Florence, biscottini di Prato, also called cantucci, *appear in shops and on restaurant menus throughout Tuscany. Why? Because they are the companion of choice for* vin santo, *the golden sweet wine that marks the end of many a Tuscan meal. At Peggy Markel's La Cucina al Focolare cooking school (page 101), chef Piero Ferrini adds an uncommon touch—a spoonful of honey—and mixes the dough directly on a marble work counter using two pastry spatulas. When serving, make sure the glasses for the accompanying* vin santo *have plenty of room for dipping.*

2 cups (11 oz/345 g) unpeeled almonds

4 large whole eggs, plus 1 large egg white

1⅔ cups (13 oz/410 g) sugar, plus more for sprinkling

1 teaspoon vanilla extract (essence)

Pinch of salt

1 teaspoon honey

Grated zest of 1 lemon

3½ cups (14 oz/440g) cake (soft-wheat) flour

1 teaspoon baking powder

1 tablespoon water

Makes about 30 biscotti

1 Preheat the oven to 350°F (180°C). Spread the almonds evenly on a baking sheet and bake, stirring occasionally, until fragrant and lightly toasted, 8–10 minutes. Remove from the oven and transfer to a large plate to cool. Leave the oven on.

2 In a large bowl, beat together the whole eggs, 1⅔ cups sugar, vanilla, and salt until smooth and creamy. Beat in the honey and lemon zest. Fold in the toasted almonds until evenly distributed.

3 In another bowl, whisk together 2½ cups (10 oz/ 315 g) of the flour and the baking powder. Use a wooden spoon to stir the flour mixture gradually into the egg mixture. When the dough becomes dense enough to handle, turn out onto a lightly floured work surface. Knead the dough gently, adding the remaining 1 cup (4 oz/125 g) flour a little bit at a time, incorporating only enough flour to hold the dough together. The dough will be moist and sticky. Form into a ball, enclose in plastic wrap, and refrigerate for 30–60 minutes. Line a baking sheet with parchment (baking) paper.

4 Transfer the dough ball to a lightly floured work surface and cut into 3 equal portions. Using lightly floured hands, roll each portion of dough into a log

about 2 inches (5 cm) wide and slightly shorter than the baking sheet. Place the logs on the baking sheet, spacing them 2–3 inches (5–7.5 cm) apart.

5 In a small bowl, whisk together the egg white and the water. Brush the tops of the logs with the egg wash and sprinkle lightly with sugar. Bake until golden, about 25 minutes. Turn off the oven and transfer the logs, still on the parchment paper, to a wire rack. Let cool for 10 minutes.

6 Transfer the logs to a cutting board and, using a large serrated knife, cut crosswise on the diagonal into slices ½ inch (12 mm) thick. Place a new piece of parchment on the baking sheet and transfer the slices to the sheet. Return to the still-warm oven for 30 minutes. Let cool completely on the baking sheet, then store in an airtight container for up to 1 month.

Serve with a fine *vin santo*.

GIORGI
SPECIALITA' ARTIGIANALI
CANTUCCI

INGREDIENTI: Farina di Grano tenero tipo "0",
Zucchero, Mandorle, Uova, Zucchero invertito,
Bicarbonato di Ammonio (polvere lievitante)
Vanillina

Prodotto da "IL CHICCO" di Giorgi Maria
nel laboratorio di Castiglion F.no (Ar)
Via Umbro Casentinese, 140

FRITTELLE DI PERE

Pear Fritters

Florentines love a well-made frittella, *or sweet fritter. Rice, ricotta cheese, and fruit (most commonly apples and pears) are all candidates for dipping in batter and frying, especially during Easter and* carnevale, *when you will see* frittelle *in the windows of many local* pasticcerie. *Savory fritters are also enjoyed. Most common are those made with chicken, rabbit, fish, and vegetables (especially artichokes, and zucchini and their flowers). The batters differ, as does the frying medium, but the results are always crisp and irresistible. The pear fritters in this recipe are at their best still warm and sprinkled with confectioners' sugar.*

1 In a large bowl, whisk together 1¾ cups (9 oz/280 g) of the flour, the granulated sugar, and the salt. Make a well in the center, add the egg yolks and olive oil, and beat the wet ingredients lightly with a fork. Switching to a wooden spoon, gradually incorporate the flour into the egg mixture, adding 1 tablespoon of the ice water at a time to the well, until the mixture forms a smooth, thick batter. You may not need all of the ice water. Cover and refrigerate for 2–3 hours.

2 In a clean bowl, using an electric mixer, beat the egg whites until they form stiff but not dry peaks. Fold the whites into the chilled batter and set aside.

3 Place the remaining ½ cup (2½ oz/75 g) flour on a plate or in a shallow bowl. Place the *vin santo* in another bowl. Dip a pear wedge in the *vin santo* and shake off the excess liquid, then dredge lightly in the flour, shake off the excess flour, and set aside on a plate. Repeat with the remaining pear wedges.

4 Pour the oil to a depth of 3–4 inches (7.5–10 cm) into a heavy-bottomed 6- to 8-inch (15- to 20-cm) saucepan, and heat to 350°F (180°C) on a deep-frying thermometer. The oil should be very hot but not smoking, and a drop of batter should sizzle upon contact with the hot oil. Working in batches to avoid crowding, use tongs to dip the pear wedges into the batter, letting the excess batter drip back into the bowl. Slip the pears into the hot oil and fry, turning once, until golden brown, about 4 minutes total. Using a wire skimmer or slotted spoon, transfer to paper towels to drain. Repeat with the remaining pears and batter, making sure the oil is at 350°F before adding the next batch. Dust with confectioners' sugar and serve at once.

Serve with a sweet white Muscat such as Moscadello di Montalcino.

2¼ cups (11½ oz/355 g) all-purpose (plain) flour

¼ cup (2 oz/60 g) granulated sugar

Pinch of salt

2 large eggs, separated, at room temperature

1 tablespoon extra-virgin olive oil

About ¾ cup (6 fl oz/180 ml) ice water

4 firm yet ripe Bosc pears, about 5 oz (155 g) each, peeled, cored, and cut into wedges ½ inch (12 mm) thick

½ cup (4 fl oz/125 ml) *vin santo*, Marsala, or other sweet wine

Corn or safflower oil for frying

Confectioners' (icing) sugar for dusting

Makes 6 servings